John Taylor

The Massoretic Text and the Ancient Versions of the Book of Micah

John Taylor

The Massoretic Text and the Ancient Versions of the Book of Micah

ISBN/EAN: 9783743409958

Manufactured in Europe, USA, Canada, Australia, Japa

Cover: Foto ©Thomas Meinert / pixelio.de

Manufactured and distributed by brebook publishing software (www.brebook.com)

John Taylor

The Massoretic Text and the Ancient Versions of the Book of Micah

WILLIAMS AND NORGATE'S LIST.

French.

Eugène's The Student's Comparative Grammar of the French Language, with an Historical Sketch of the Formation of French. For the use of Public Schools. With Exercises. By G. EUGÈNE-FASNACHT, French Master, Westminster School. 12th Edition, thoroughly revised. Square crown 8vo. cloth 5s

Or, Grammar, 3s ; Exercises, 2s 6d.

"The appearance of a Grammar like this is in itself a sign that great advance is being made in the teaching of modern as well as of ancient languages...... The rules and observations are all scientifically classified and explained."—*Educational Times.*

"In itself this is in many ways the most satisfactory Grammar for beginners that we have as yet seen."—*Athenæum.*

Eugène's French Method. Elementary French Lessons. Easy Rules and Exercises preparatory to the "Student's Comparative French Grammar." By the same Author. 11th Edition. Crown 8vo. cloth 1s 6d

"Certainly deserves to rank among the best of our Elementary French Exercise-books."—*Educational Times.*

"To those who begin to study French, I may recommend, as the best book of the kind with which I am acquainted, '*Eugène's Elementary Lessons in French.*' "—*Dr. Breymann, Lecturer of the French Language and Literature, Owens College, Manchester.*

The Student's Graduated French Reader, for the use of Public Schools. I. First Year. Anecdotes, Tales, Historical Pieces. Edited with Notes and a Complete Vocabulary by LEON DELBOS, M.A., of King's College, London. 7th Ed. Crown 8vo. cloth 2s

The Student's Second French Reader. By the same. 4th Ed. Crown 8vo. cloth 2s

Lemaistre (J.) French for Beginners. Lessons Systematic, Practical and Etymological. By J. LEMAISTRE. 2nd Edition. Crown 8vo. 2s

Eugène's French Reader for Beginners. 2nd Edition. Anecdotes and Tales. Edited, with Notes and a complete Vocabulary, by Leon Delbos, M.A. 2nd Ed. Crown 8vo. cloth 1s 6d

Roget (F. F.) Introduction to Old French. History, Grammar, Chrestomathy, Glossary. Cloth 6s

Tarver. Colloquial French, for School and Private Use. By H. Tarver, B.-ès-L., late of Eton College. 328 pp. Crown 8vo. cloth 5s

Victor Hugo. Les Misérables. Les Principaux Episodes. Edited, with Life and Notes, by J. Boïelle, Senior French Master, Dulwich College. 2nd Ed. 2 vols. Crown 8vo. cloth each 3s 6d

Victor Hugo. **Notre Dame de Paris.** Adopted for the use of Schools and Colleges. By J. Boïelle, B.A., Senior French Master, Dulwich College. 2 vols. Crown 8vo. cloth — each 3s

Foa (Mad. Eugen.) **Contes Historiques,** with idiomatic Notes by G. A. NEVEU. Third Edition. Cloth — 2s

Larochejacquelein (Madame de) **Scenes from the War in the Vendée.** Edited from her Memoirs in French, with Introduction and Notes, by C. SCUDAMORE, M.A. Oxon. Crown 8vo. cloth — 2s

Krueger (H.) **Short but Comprehensive French Grammar.** 7th Edition. 180 pp. 12mo. cloth — 2s

Boïelle. **French Composition** through Lord Macaulay's English. I. Frederic the Great, Edited with Notes, Hints, and Introduction, by JAMES BOÏELLE, B.A. (Univ. Gall.), Senior French Master, Dulwich College, &c., &c. Crown 8vo. cloth — 3s

—— II. Warren Hastings. Crown 8vo. cloth — 3s 6d

—— III. Lord Clive — 3s

Delbos (L.) **French Accidence and Minor Syntax.** 2nd Edition. Crown 8vo. cloth — 1s 6d

—— **Student's French Composition** on an entirely new plan. Crown 8vo. cloth — 3s 6d

Roussy. **Cours de Versions.** Pieces for translation into French, with Notes. Crown 8vo. cloth — 2s 6d

Vinet (A.) **Chrestomathie Française ou Choix de Morceaux** tirés des meilleurs Ecrivains Français. 11th Edition. 358 pp. cloth — 3s 6d

Williams (T. S.) and J. Lafont. **French Commercial Correspondence.** A Collection of Modern Mercantile Letters in French and English, with their translation on opposite pages. 2nd Edition. 12mo. cloth — 4s 6d

French Classics for English Schools. Edited with Introduction and Notes by LEON DELBOS, M.A., late of King's College. Crown 8vo. cloth

1. Racine. Les Plaideurs — 1s 6d
2. Corneille. Horace — 1s 6d
3. Corneille. Cinna — 1s 6d
4. Molière. Bourgeois Gentilhomme — 1s 6d
5. Corneille. Le Cid — 1s 6d
6. Molière, Les Précieuses Ridicules. — 1s 6d
7. Chateaubriand. Voyage en Amérique — 1s 6d
8. De Maistre. Les Prisonniers du Caucase, and le Lépreux d'Aoste — 1s 6d
9. La Fontaine's Select Fables. — 1s 6d
10. Molière. Le Misanthrope. By G. H. CLARKE — 1s 6d

(*To be continued.*)

Fleury's Histoire de France, racontée à la Jeunesse, edited for the use of English Pupils, with Grammatical Notes by Beljame. 3rd Edition. 12mo. cloth boards 3s 6d
Mandrou (A.) French Poetry for English Schools. 2nd Edition. 12mo. cloth 2

German.

Weisse's Complete Practical Grammar of the German Language, with Exercises in Conversations, Letters &c. 4th Edition. Entirely re-written. 12mo. cloth 6
—— New Conversational Exercises in German Composition, 2nd Edition. 12mo. cloth (Key, 5s) 3s 6d
Schlutter's German Class Book. A Course of Instruction based on Becker's System, and so arranged as to exhibit the Self-development of the Language, and its Affinities with the English. By Fr. Schlutter, Royal Military Academy, Woolwich. 4th Edition. 12mo. cloth (Key 5s) 5
Möller (A.) A German Reading Book. A Companion to Schlutter's German Class Book. With a complete Vocabulary. 150 pp. 12mo. cloth 2
Ravensberg (A. v.) Practical Grammar of the German Language. Conversational Exercises, Dialogues and Idiomatic Expressions. Third Edition. 12mo. cloth (Key, 2s) 5
—— Rose's English into German. A Selection of Anecdotes, Stories, &c., with copious Notes. 2nd Edition. Cloth (Key, 5s) 4s 6d
—— German Reader, Prose and Poetry, with copious Notes for Beginners. 2nd Edition. Crown 8vo. cloth 3
Ohly (Dr. C. H.) Manual of German Composition, with Passages for translation. Crown 8vo. cloth 3s 6d
Hein (G.) German Examination Papers. Comprising a Complete set of German Papers set at the Local Examinations in the four Universities of Scotland. Crown 8vo. cloth 2s 6d
Ahn's German Method by Rose. A New Edition of the genuine Book, with a Supplement consisting of Model of Conjugations, a Table of Verbs, Rules, &c. &c. By A. V. Rose. 2 Courses in 1 vol. Cloth 3s 6d
—— German Method by Rose, &c. First Course. Cloth 2
Apel's Short and Practical German Grammar for Beginners with copious Examples and Exercises. 2nd Edition. 12mo. cloth 2s 6

For Continuation see the end of the Volume.

THE MASSORETIC TEXT

AND THE

ANCIENT VERSIONS

OF

THE BOOK OF MICAH.

BY

JOHN TAYLOR, M.A. (LOND.).

Καὶ εἰ μὲν καλῶς καὶ εὐθίκτως τῇ συντάξει τοῦτο καὶ αὐτὸς ἤθελον· εἰ δὲ εὐτελῶς καὶ μετρίως τοῦτο ἐφικτὸν ἦν μοι.—2 MACC. xv. 38.

WILLIAMS AND NORGATE,
14, HENRIETTA STREET, COVENT GARDEN, LONDON;
AND 20, SOUTH FREDERICK STREET, EDINBURGH.
1890

PREFACE.

In the writer of an essay on the text of Micah it would be mere affectation to profess that he has attacked the subject without knowing, and to some extent being affected by, the views of others. He would at the outset lie open to the pertinent inquiry into the reason for his selecting this particular portion of the Old Testament. The present writer was fully aware of the existence of two directly opposed opinions, one of which holds the Massoretic Text to be in an extremely unsatisfactory state, whilst the other maintains that it has undergone but little corruption. But it seemed to him quite feasible to work out his own conclusions by careful observation of the phenomena presented by the current Hebrew Text and the Ancient Versions, and then to reconsider those conclusions in the light of the various results which his predecessors have obtained. In this way a substantial independence would be secured whilst the unpardonable presumption would be avoided of leaving unnoticed the work already done. The consequence of this reference to the criticisms of others has in some cases been the alteration or modification of the views adopted and in others the retention and defence of them. Ryssel's " Untersuchungen über die Textgestalt und die Echtheit des Buches Micha" calls for special mention in this connection. Much of the matter found in these notes is also to be found in Ryssel. But it is believed that the difference between the modes in which this common matter is handled in the two essays respectively will sufficiently prove that the remarks common to both have not been borrowed. No two men can traverse the same ground on the same quest without being struck by the same prominent features, and it would have been an unworthy yielding to the fear of being accused of plagiarism to delete what had been written on finding that it had been in greater or less part anticipated.

The result of the inquiry into the character of the Massoretic Text needs hardly any other setting forth than that which is supplied by the lists of proposed emendations which are printed at the close. They indicate the belief that this text is in many passages corrupt, that the ancient Versions supply a considerable amount of help in restoring the original, and that where these fail conjectural emendations are open to us. To this, however, it must be added that in more than one instance it is impossible to arrive at anything like assured conviction.

The course of the inquiry brings out the fact that the LXX ought not to be credited with so overwhelming an influence over the other Versions as is frequently ascribed to it. To mention first the Peshiṭta. The late lamented Dr. Hatch, in his "Essays in Biblical Greek," p. 133, says: "The Latin and Eastern Versions of the Old Testament were made not from the Hebrew original but from the LXX Version," and on the same page includes the Syriac amongst these Eastern Versions. This is a mere *obiter dictum*, but unless corrected it may prove misleading. Leaving aside all consideration of the other books of Scripture it would be quite enough to read together the Peshiṭta and the Arabic of this book of Micah—the latter being confessedly a translation of the LXX—to compel the conclusion that the former, though greatly influenced by the highly esteemed Greek Version, is none the less a translation from the Hebrew. But it is necessary to go further. More than once Ryssel uses such language as that on p. 100: "die Pesch. wie sonst abhängig von LXX sein könnte." That "wie sonst" is not justified by the facts. It might almost be laid down as a rule that where there is a real difficulty in the text the LXX and the Peshiṭta each pursue their own way. Geiger's characterization of the Version as a whole, " zum ueberwiegenden Theile nach dem Urtexte abgefasst", if qualified by the remark he elsewhere makes, " Der Syrer folgt hier, wie häufig in den Proph., den 70," is not far from the truth. Sebök, also, "Die syrische Uebersetzung der zwölf Kleinen Propheten," is undoubtedly justified when, in the Introduction, he lays stress on "die Zahlreichen und starken Berührungen mit dem gewöhnlichen judischen Targum." No account of the Peshiṭta would be correct which left this unmentioned.

With some modification a similar *caveat* might be entered against the terms in which the connection between the Vulgate and the LXX has been spoken of. Hatch's words, quoted above, do not draw the needful distinction between the Old Latin, which was made from the LXX, and the Vulgate. And Ryssel says, on vi. 7, "die Vulgata wie sonst von den LXX abhängig ist." No doubt the influence of the LXX on the Vulg. is deep and pervasive. But the best corrective of unduly strong language on the subject is supplied by Jerome's Commentaries, where the Vulg. is printed along with his translation of the LXX, and the many discrepancies between the two are patent; where also, as well in his treatment of important Hebrew words as in the general course of his task, the great father is seen to be striving after results which shall be "juxta Hebraicam veritatem."

As a rule this essay has taken no account of the Arabic save when that translation forsakes the guidance of the LXX for that of the Peshiṭta, or when its renderings have some bearing on the various readings of the Greek Codices. Observations on the latter point confirm the already well-established fact that the type of text usually followed by the Arabic translator is that represented in the Codex Alexandrinus, and this the more markedly when the divergences of this codex from the Vatican MS. proceed from design and not from mere clerical errors. Most of the questions arising out of these divergences must be decided in favour of the Vatican.

From the textual critic's point of view the Targum is singularly disappointing. Much might have been expected from the linguistic tact of native paraphrasts writing in a cognate dialect. But there is scarcely a difficulty which the Targumists have not evaded, and the points at which one is most anxious to be sure what their text was are the ones where we are reduced to utter uncertainty. On the other hand the so-called Targum of Jonathan can never fail to be interesting as one landmark on the line of Jewish thought, or, perhaps, it would be more correct to speak of it as exhibiting many successive landmarks; for there are in it elements belonging to many ages. An early writer would not have dared explicitly to name Rome as it is named in the Codex Reuchlinianus at chap. vii. 10.

In a considerable number of instances it has seemed desirable to point out mistakes in the Latin translations which are given in the London Polyglot. No attempt has been made to enumerate all that occur. But the true sense of the Versions is so frequently obscured in the Latin renderings that it behoves everyone who notes this to do his part in indicating the danger of an implicit reliance on the translations.

Working for the most part at a distance from the great libraries involves the disadvantage of having few books available. For the Hebrew text Baer and Delitzsch's Edition has been consulted, as well as the London Polyglot and Athias: for the LXX the Polyglot, and Tischendorf's Fourth Edition: for the Vulgate the Polyglot, Heyse and Tischendorf's Edition with the readings of the Codex Amiatinus, and Martianay's Edition of Jerome's Commentaries: for the Targum, Peshitta and Arabic the Polyglot. The letters *a, b, r,* used for designating the various readings of the Targum, are taken from Cornill, who employs them respectively for the Antwerp Polyglot, the Bomberg-Buxtorf Edition, and the Codex Reuchlinianus. His collation of these, so far as they relate to the prophets, is given at pp. 178-202, "Zeitschrift für die Alttestamentliche Wissenschaft," 1887. Unfortunately this collation is not to be relied on. "Unterschiede, wie beispielweise איתרחיץ : יתרחיץ, מסרבן: סרבן, לדבית ישראל : לבית ישראל, לביני : ביני, לארעא : על ארעא דיכין : דנן sind in das folgende Verzeichniss nicht aufgenommen:" that is the principle acted on; and it is a radically mistaken one. It is impossible for a collator to determine beforehand the value or valuelessness of any given variation: that is a point which can only be decided when the document comes to be used for critical purposes. Hence every variation, however slight, should be noted. Codex Reuchlinianus contains a considerable number of various readings, some of them of real importance, which are not mentioned by Cornill.

The following signs and abbreviations have been employed:—

    M. T. for Massoretic Text.
    Targ. „ Targum.
    Ar. „ Arabic.
    Vulg. „ Vulgate.
    Cod. Amiat. „ Codex Amiatinus of the Vulg.
    Jer. „ Jerome: or, where the reference is to the Greek text, Jerome's rendering of the LXX.
    Comm. „ Jerome's Commentaries, particularly the one on Micah.
    Lond. Polyg. „ The London Polyglot.
    Field „ Field's Edition of Origen's Hexapla, from which are quoted Aquila, Symmachus, and Theodotion, as Aq., Symm., and Theod. respectively.
    A. „ Codex Alexandrinus of the LXX.
    B. „ Codex Vaticanus of the LXX.

    When MSS. of the LXX are referred to by means of numbers, these numbers are the ones used in Holmes and Parsons' "*Vet. Test. Graec. &c.*"

    Pesh. „ Peshiṭta.
    Rich. „ a MS. of the Pesh. in the British Museum, called Rich, 7152, in the Catalogue, and there described as "pervetustus et quantivis pretii."

Add. for a MS. of the Pesh. in the British Museum, called Add. 18,715, and said by Dr. Wright to be by a good hand of the twelfth century.

Eg. „ a MS. of the Pesh. in the British Museum, called Egerton 704, assigned by Dr. Wright to the seventeenth century.

Ewald's Lehrbuch d. Heb. Sprache, and Davies' English translation of Gesenius' Heb. Grammar are referred to as Ewald and Ges. respectively.

BORROWDALE VICARAGE,
September 23rd, 1890.

THE MASSORETIC TEXT

OF THE

BOOK OF MICAH.

———◆———

CHAPTER I.

V. 1. No alteration.

The LXX, καὶ ἐγένετο λόγος, κ.τ.λ., implies the reading ויהי דבר יהוה וגו' which appears to have been substituted for דבר יהוה אשר היה וגו' because of the cumbrousness of the text in which דבר יהוה אשר ח' after a long interval has to be taken up again by אשר חזה. The adoption of this reading, however, did not enable the LXX to produce a well-knit sentence: their καὶ ἐγ. λ. κυρίου . . . . ὑπὲρ ὧν εἶδε, κ.τ.λ.—where ὑπὲρ ὧν is probably due to unwillingness to construe the noun of hearing to which אשר refers with חזה the verb of seeing—is not at all more satisfactory than the M. T. That a various reading should be found in the superscription is not surprising, seeing that this would be drawn up by the editor or editors and would therefore be looked upon as more open to emendation than the words of the prophet himself. But there can be no hesitation in preferring the M. T. The other Verss. all support it: ויהי וגו' would better suit a second part, or an intermediate member of a series, than an independent work, and none of the prophets save Jonah, which is a narrative rather than a prophecy, commence thus.

דבר יהוה אשר היה .... אשר חזה results from a mixture of two constructions, דבר אשר היה אל, Hosea i. 1, and חזון אשר חזה, Isa. i. 1: at Amos i. 1, we have a very similar heading, דבר עמוס .... אשר חזה. Here, as at Hagg. ii. 21 and Zech. i. 1, vii. 4, for אל the Targ. has עם and the Pesh. ܠ. The prepositions are rendered by the Verss. with great freedom. To the ܠ ܥܠ of the Pesh. the פתגמא על of the Aramaic passages, Ezra iv. 7, v. 11, furnishes an exact parallel.

המרשתי. The LXX missed the customary mention of the father's name, found in such passages as Hosea i. 1, "Hosea, son of Beeri": it therefore treated הם׳ as a patronymic, τὸν τοῦ Μωρασθεὶ (varr. lec. Μωραθεὶ, Μωραθὶ, Μωραθίτην). At Jer. xxvi. 18 it has ὁ Μωραθίτης. The Targ. in both passages has מָרֵשָׁה and the Pesh. agrees with this, against the LXX, in treating the word as derived from the name of a town, although it spells it here ܡܪܫܢ and there ܡܪܫܢ. The renderings of these two Versions, which would imply the reading מָרֵשָׁתִי or מְרֵשָׁתִי, are to be accounted for by their having identified מורשת גת, v. 14, and מרשה, v. 15. The evidence of the M. T. and the LXX in favour of מָרֵשָׁתִי outweighs theirs. This is one of the instances which remind s that the Ar. was to some extent influenced by the Pesh., for whilst we here have موراني in accordance with the LXX, at Jer. xxvi. 18 its المارناني is after the Pesh. The σ, which fails to appear in many codices, was omitted because of its similarity in sound to θ.

The sing. βασιλέως, of A, 36, 62, 106, 147, Ar., meets with no support in any other Vers., and the probability that it is a mere error of transcription is enhanced by the fact that 95 and 185*, which also read the sing., have τῶν before it.

The Targ. on this verse paraphrases דבר יהוה by פתגם נבואה מן קדם יי, inserts דבית before יהודה, and rids itself of any difficulty respecting חזה by using אתנבי. It does not agree with Pesh., which probably follows LXX, in repeating על before ירושלם: the Ar. here forsakes its models; it, also, having no preposition.

V. 2. No alteration.

שמעו עמים כלם. LXX ἀκούσατε λαοὶ λόγους. The correspondence of the two clauses ש'ע'כ' and הקשיבי ארץ ומלאה is strongly in favour of the M. T., as is also the fact that "Hear *words*, O ye peoples," is an expression which we do not usually find in the Bible; Deut. xxxii. 1, mentioned by Ryssel, is not a parallel: ἀκουέτω .... ῥήματα ἐκ στόματός μου; the ἐκ στ. μου makes all the difference. Targ. כלהון and Pesh. ܟܠܒܡ also support M. T. With regard to the change from the third to the second pers. in the Pesh., it need only be said that it does not rest on a text differing from the Massoretic: at Job xvii. 10, the Pesh. has made the same alteration. On the use of the third pers. in exclamations, see Ewald § 327, 1*a*, and Driver, Heb. Tenses, § 198, Obs. The Pesh. itself has been forced to recognise the third pers. in מלאה of the next clause.

For כלם the LXX cannot have read קלים: against such a supposition there is the difference in sound between כ and ק and the further consideration that the plu. of קול is קלות. Nor did they actually read מלים, or *defective* מלם. But it is quite possible that they thought כלם ought to be מלם: like the Pesh., they may have been offended with the suffix of the third pers. The suggestion that they supplied the appropriate object after שמעו would not account for their leaving, on this theory, the word כלם untranslated. And the objection to their having thought of מלה that it belongs to the stock of Aramaic words, and, consequently, is not to be ascribed to a writer of Micah's period is beside the mark. Aramaic words were in sufficiently familiar use at the period when the LXX translation was made.

The LXX alone turns the abstract ומלאה into the concrete καὶ πάντες οἱ ἐν αὐτῇ. The Pesh. ܟܒܥܐ gives the sense with sufficient accuracy, the כ being that of accompaniment.

אדני יהוה. A, followed by Ar., has only one κύριος. This is partly to be accounted for by LXX having to translate two Heb. words by the same Greek word. In some passages, however, where they have another suitable word available, as in Ps. xxxi. 5, יהוה אל they have κύριος once only. Cf. also Ps. lxxxiv. 11, B; Isa. xxviii. 22, lxv. 15 and Isa. l. 7, A. The Targ. here has מימרא דיי אלהים; Pesh. "Lord of Lords"; Vulg. Dominus Deus.

לעד is rendered in LXX εἰς μαρτύριον, a sense which the word not unfrequently bears, though it is not suitable here. Jerome's comment is "Sive ut in Hebraico legitur, *in testem*, velut apertius interpretatus est Symmachus, *testificans*. "Ἄλλος· εἰς μάρτυρα." Field.

LXX, Pesh. and Vulg., with some Heb. Codd., have ו before הקשיבי: the Verss. very frequently supply this conjunction; the Codd. referred to have also the plu. of the verb הקשיבו; this has originated, quite unnecessarily, from the desire to provide a plu. verb for the pair of nouns.

V. 3. No alteration.

יצא ממקמו is rendered in the Targ. מאתר בית שכנתיה מתגלי. The coming forth is rightly interpreted as a self-revelation. We might have thought that the Targ. read יצא a second time in place of ירד in the next clause, seeing that it again uses יתגלי, were it not that all the other Verss. agree with the M. T., and that the two words are not sufficiently alike to be readily confounded.

A, not followed by Ar., omits καὶ καταβήσεται. The words are so similar to καὶ ἐπιβήσεται that they may have been omitted by accident: on the other hand the apparent contradiction to καὶ ἐπιβ. which they involve may have led to their being dropped. If the latter be the true explanation ירד was probably looked upon as a duplicate of דרך.

The Polyg. *conculcabit* is too strong a translation of the Ar. word here used: at Ps. xci. 12, the more suitable *calcabis* is employed.

The Targ. תוקפי ארעא for במותי ארץ was no doubt chosen to indicate that the "high-places" here intended are not those on which sacrifices were offered.

V. 4. No alteration.

καὶ σαλευθήσεται τὰ ὄρη .... καὶ αἱ κοιλάδες τακήσονται. For והעמקים יתבקעו and ונמסו ההרים the LXX read ויתבקעו ההרים and והעמקים נמסו. Whether they actually found this in their text or themselves introduced it there is not clear. In either case it is not the original order. The M. T. is supported by the other Verss. The motive of the change has obviously been to bring κηρός and τήκω together, as they are found in so many passages. And the parallelism is better kept in the M. T., where the first member of the first half of the verse corresponds to the first of the second half.

σαλευθήσεται does not seem a good rendering of יתבקעו, but it is used for so many Heb. words, התפלץ, מטה, חול, &c., that we are under no necessity of thinking that it implies a different reading here. The Ar. is no doubt right in taking it to mean a leaping *for fear*, as it so often does in LXX.

Jerome's *consumentur* for נמסו is very inadequate. The Comm. shows that he felt it so:—"Consumentur sive tabescent." The *et* before *aquae* in the common text of the Vulg. is not found in Cod. Amiat. or in the Comm. It crept into the Vulg. through the influence of the LXX, the latter Vers., with the Pesh., having inserted it for the sake of explicitness. Such cases as *decurrunt* and بذِي for the passive מֻגָּרִים remind us that we are not to look for the exact reproduction in the Verss. of Voices, Numbers, &c.; the same is to be said of the LXX sing. ὕδωρ for מים.

V. 5. For חַטֹּאות probably read חַטַּאת and for בְּמוֹת read חַטַּאת בֵּית.

The Massoretic note directs that חטאות be written *plene*. With this the Vulg., Pesh. and *r* of the Targ. agree. The common text of the Targ. has the sing. חטא and the LXX has ἁμαρτίαν. The value of the evidence borne by the Pesh. is discounted by its reading the sing. in the place corresponding to this in the second half of the verse, and that of the Targ. is diminished by its treating פשע as plu., in opposition to all the other Verss. No doubt the word was originally written *defective*, and the LXX regarded it as sing. on account of the parallelism: this reason, though not quite decisive, has much force in it, and since it is probable that the Massoretes were influenced by the plu. במות (on which see below), we should be inclined to agree with the LXX.

The plu. πάντα ταῦτα of the LXX, which in the Pesh. is made yet more emphatic by being placed at the head of the sentence, brings out the plu. force which the context shows to belong to כל־זאת.

The use of מי in this verse is not satisfactorily explained by Ewald, § 325. He says that the distinction between it and מה is always observed, and that מי always inquires after the *person*, not the *thing*, even when the language used does not express this. Pusey makes the same assertion: "מי always relates to a personal object, and apparent exceptions may be reduced to this. So AE, Kim. Tanch. Poc." Sebök, on the other hand, points out that the Massora remarks that these two particles are used the one for the other, and he refers to Ginsburg's edition of the

Massora I. 596, "where it is observed that the מדנהאי read מי for מה". This, however, should not lead us, with Sebök, to substitute מה for מי in the text. The distinction between the two may not have been recognised by Micah. And the presence of מי is the best explanation of the turn which the Targ. gives to the expression:— " Where did they of the house of Jacob sin, &c. ?"

In the two halves of the verse the two pairs of names are not kept precisely parallel : Jacob and Israel in the first are followed by Jacob and Judah in the second, the Jacob in this second pair being connected with Samaria, and the Judah with Jerusalem ; as though Jacob signified the Northern Kingdom, and Judah, instead of being sharply distinguished from Israel, were identical with it. We are not justified in substituting Israel for Jacob in the second of these pairs, as Sebök would do, on the ground that the Massora calls attention to the interchange of Judah with Israel, e.g. at Ezek. xxv. 8. The Verss. all agree with our M. T., and the explanation of the sudden appearance of Judah here is that Jerusalem, its capital city, was to be mentioned in answer to the question.

ומי במות יהודה. The Vulg. is the only Vers. which read במות. The Pesh. has "And what is the sin of Judah?" The Targ. here, as in the foregoing clause, uses a verb, but it is the verb חטו. The LXX has καὶ τίς ἡ ἁμαρτία οἴκου Ἰούδα. Their reading evidently was ומי חטאת בית יהודה, corresponding to the ובחטאת בית ישראל above. This reading would explain both the M. T. and the Verss. It entirely agrees with the Targ.; it differs from the Pesh. only by having בית, and this the

Pesh. may have omitted for the sake of conformity to the immediately preceding clause, מִי פֶּשַׁע יַעֲקֹב.* In the margin, opposite חַטֹּאת בֵּית יְהוּדָה, an explanatory בָּמוֹת might be inserted; nothing being more likely to suggest itself as the crowning sin of Judah than the erection of high-places in the city which the Lord chose to set His Name there. Through its similarity in form to בֵּית this marginal בָּמוֹת took its place, and the now superfluous חַטֹּאת was rejected.† The unanswerable argument in favour of the LXX is that the question מִי בָּמוֹת יְהוּדָה cannot be replied to by הֲלוֹא יְרוּשָׁלָיִם.

The Targ. obtains complete symmetry in its rendering of this verse, not only by its use of two plurals where the Heb. has only one, but also by inserting בֵּית before each proper noun:—" For the transgressions of the house of Jacob is all this, and for the sins of the house of Israel. Where have they of the house of Jacob transgressed? Is it not in Samaria? And where have they of the house of Judah sinned? Is it not in Jerusalem?"

V. 6. No alteration.

וְשַׂמְתִּי שֹׁמְרוֹן לְעִי הַשָּׂדֶה. LXX Καὶ θήσομαι Σαμάρειαν

---

* Cod. A of the LXX has secured parallelism in just the opposite way, inserting οἴκου before Ἰακώβ. The Ar. does not follow it here, but Jerome's text of the LXX agrees with it. Possibly the οἴκου may have originated in a scribe's error, ιατου Ιακωβ being read as οικου Ιακωβ.

† The reading in Symmachus: "τίνα τὰ ὑψηλά, Syro-Hex., ܐܡܚܡ ܐܢܐ ܢܣܒ (Field), shows that this corruption of the Heb. text occurred at an early date.

εἰς ὀπωροφυλάκιον* ἀγροῦ. Cod. A ὡς ὀπ. The Ar. does not follow A. At iii. 12, where עִי is not preceded by לְ, A has εἰς and B ὡς. As עִי in this passage, so עִיִּין in iii. 12, and עִיִּים Ps. lxxix. 1, are rendered ὀπωροφ. Fuerst explains this by saying that in these three passages they incorrectly read עִיר, 'a watcher,' which is found in Dan. iv. 10, 14, 20. There is something to be said for this, though it is not quite satisfactory. By the ear עִי and עִיר might easily be confounded, and the plu. of עִי does not look unlike עִיר. But it is difficult to believe that the LXX committed the same blunder in three passages : עִיר, in the sense mentioned above, is a word so rarely used that it is scarcely likely the LXX would think of it here, unless compelled to do so : עִיר, moreover, does not mean ὀπωρ.; in Dan. it is rendered ἄγγελος. At Isa. i. 8, and xxiv. 20, ὀπ. is the translation of מְלוּנָה, and it may be fairly taken that whilst the LXX were aware that עִי has not quite so specific a meaning as ὀπ, they thought themselves justified in translating thus, because of the similarity in tone and scope of the Isaiah and the Micah passages. There is nothing helpful in Hitzig's suggestion that the LXX conjectured עִיר for עִי in the sense in which the former word is used at Isa. i. 8: and that they should have so conjectured is most unlikely, seeing that מְלוּנָה is the word there rendered ὀπ. For the rest of Hitzig's conjecture: "Man lese עָיָה, so dass לְ vor מַטָּעֵי den Accus. des Obj. einführe indem die const. wie Am. 5, 17 gewechselt wird. Also: *zum Felde* d.i. zur Wildniss (vgl. z. B.

---

* Aq. εἰς σωρούς, Symm. and Theod. εἰς βουνούς.

1 Mos. 25, 27) die Weinbergpflanzungen, welche vorzugsweise Culturland;" it may safely be said that the result does not justify the change, the text thus obtained meaning rather, "I will make a field into plantations," than "I will make plantations into a field."

The Pesh. (wrongly translated *in arvum ruris* in the Polyg.) follows the LXX, ܟܡܐ ܕܟܢܐ ܕܚܩܠܐ. As illustrating the connection between this Vers. and the Ar. it may be noted that whereas here both agree with the LXX, at Isa. i. 8, and xxiv. 20, where the Pesh. adopts another rendering the Ar. follows it.

The Targ. here has a double rendering. For

ושמתי ש' לעי הש' למטעי כרם

it gives

ואשוי ש' לינרי חקלן בית צדות מצבת כרם

The two points which challenge attention are the superfluousness of בית צדות and the omission of ל before מצבת. The best way of accounting for these is to assume that the older Targ. was בית צדות חקלן, corresponding pretty closely to the Pesh. ܟܡܐ ܕܟܢܐ ܕܚܩܠܐ, and that לינרי was an alternative, inserted later in the margin. This alternative, being nearer to the Heb. than the older rendering, found its way into the text, without, however, entirely ousting ב' צ', which were now placed after לינרי ח', and their insertion in this position caused the loss of ל before מצבת. Some confirmation of this connexion between בית צ' and עי is furnished by לצדו being the Targ. on Ps. lxxix. 1 for לעיים. Ryssel takes an altogether diffe-

rent view:—" Um die Weinbergpflanzung unmissverständlich als Verwüstungsstätte ... zu kennzeichnen, hat der Targumist die Worte כרם למטעי paraphrisirt durch [ich will machen Samaria] *zu der Verwüstungsstätte des Weinbergs* (denn בית צדוה ist stat. constr.) oder (wenn dafür gelesen wird בית צדותא im stat. emph. oder auch בית צדו im stat. abs.): [ich will machen] zu einer Verwüstungsstätte die Weinbergpflanzungen." There are two considerations in favour of this view:—
1. צדות is in the construct. Ryssel himself, however, places no reliance on the reading, and is prepared to accept either the emphatic or the absolute, nay, is forced to adopt one of these if the better of his two ways of arranging the words is to stand. 2. In that way two corresponding pairs of words are secured:—Samaria, a heap; vineyard plantations, a place of desolation. But to justify this, ל should have stood before מצבת as it does before יגרי. So far as the first of the two alternatives is concerned its heaviness and clumsiness would render it suspicious. And, on the whole, without dogmatizing respecting the precise relations between the Targ. and the Pesh., we are justified in believing that the בית צ' of the one did not belong to a different clause from the ܟܪ, ܒܬ of the other.

The Vulg. turns למטעי כרם by a circumstantial clause: "cum plantatur vinea." It is not quite clear whether Jer. recognized the plu. or not: amongst his comments both "in plantationem vineae" and "in plantationem vinearum" occur. The other Verss. agree in having the sing., probably because the plu. seemed difficult to understand.* Vineyard plantations, however, are more in place here than a vineyard plantation. At Isa. lx. 21, on the other hand, the sing. of the Kethib gives a better sense than the plu. of the Qeri. In our passage, as in so many others, the LXX and the Pesh. avoid the asyndeton, inserting καὶ before φυτείας.

והגרתי לני אבניה. LXX Καὶ κατασπάσω εἰς χάος, κ.τ.λ., of which the Ar., "And I will cast her stones into *an open plain*," is a weak rendering. The Pesh. ܘܐܒܢܝ betrays the influence of κατασπάσω, but its ܟܢܝ̈ܫܐ is a rendering of לגל. This simple explanation is to be preferred to Ryssel's cumbrous one: he says that Pesh. connected הגיר with the Syr. noun ܟܢܝ̈ܫܐ because they have the root *gar* in common, and that taking הגיר thus in the sense of "to heap together," they took לני, without alteration, as meaning "a heap." But this is arbitrary treatment of ני. The LXX would seem to have vocalized לְנֵי: M. T., Targ. and Pesh. לַגַּי is better; the stones of the city will be thrown into *the* valley which is close at hand.

V. 7. קִבְּצוּ for קִבְצָה.

Targ., Pesh. and Vulg. agree with M. T. in the passive forms יכתו and ישרפו; LXX has actives: no indication has been given as to who the agents are, and therefore, although the active is not impossible, the M. T. is to be followed.

---

* "In plantationes," the Polyg. translation of the Targ. מצבת, is one of the many illustrations of the extent to which the renderings of one Vers. affected those of another: it is the translation of the Heb. which has led to this plu.

אתנניה is rendered by Pesh. ܂ܢܐܓ̈ܪܐ, and by Targ. טעותהא: they were led to this by the parallel פסיליה. In the second half of the verse Pesh. has the correct ܐܓܪܐ both times, and the Targ., which agrees with it the first time, gives a very good paraphrase of the meaning, לבית פלחי טעותא. In this second half the M. T. has the sing. אתנן both times; the Targ. has sing. in the first place, and affords no indication of the number which it recognised in the second; Pesh. has the sing. twice; LXX has plu. both times; Vulg. has plu. in the first, following the LXX, but, adopting a different preposition from the LXX, it turns to the sing. in the second case. There is no need to suppose that the LXX read the plu.: after the plu. in the first half of the verse it would seem more natural; in any case אתנן is a collective; with the abstract πορνεία, their rendering of זונה, it was more suitable.

Very probably the word קבצה has arisen out of קִבְּצוּ וְ: Targ., Pesh. and Vulg. all treat it so; that the verb here should be in the plu. corresponding to the parallel ישובו is not unlikely, and the LXX has shown its sense of this parallelism by making both verbs sing.; Ewald § 131, 1, d, points out that in the Hophal *u* is sometimes sharpened into *i*, and adds "קבצה Mikha i. 7, wäre als pass. auch wegen des *a* der zweiten sylbe wirklich passender (es ward gesammelt); einige handschriften lesen wirklich קֻבְּ'." It may be doubted whether there is any exception to the rule that the Piel in pause always has the perfect ē, and this would seem to show that the Massoretes at all events suspected that the Pual was found here. For ישובו LXX has substituted תשיב, led to this by the belief that this final clause is parallel to the one preceding it: for עד they may possibly have thought על the true reading. The Ar. has taken their ἐκ in the sense of "because of," and in order to get as strong a sense as possible has rendered συνέστρεψεν by the very forcible اكسفت (subvertetur).

In the first clause of this verse Cod. Reuch. has the reading ידקקון for the ידקרון of *a* and *b*: no doubt it is correct; דקר is very rare and means "to pierce," whereas דקק, "to break in pieces," is the sense required.

Cod. Amiat. has *igni*, so also the Comment.

V. 8. No alteration.

M. T. and Vulg. have all the verbs in the 1st pers. sing.; Pesh. in 2nd pers. sing. fem. imper., referring to Samaria; LXX in 3rd pers. sing. indic., also referring to Samaria; Targ. in 3rd pers. masc. plu.: the translators could not understand the introduction of verbs in the 1st pers. into the midst of a passage where the 3rd prevails; each followed his own view as to the precise change required. Καὶ ποιήσαιτε of A· is the result of a scribe's error: after ποιήσεται had been written ποιήσαιτε through itacism, the καὶ was inserted to introduce what now appeared to be a verb in a different number and mood from the foregoing.

The Kethib שׁילל is preferable to the Qeri שׁולל: the former occurs nowhere else, and it would be natural to alter it into the common form, whereas the י is easily to be accounted for by the desire for assonance, אילכה, שׁילל, ואילילה. To this desire we must certainly refer the י in אילכה, a form which the verb does not elsewhere assume, although analogies to it are not infrequent: Hitzig refers to איתם, Ps. xix. 4, תיעשה, Ex. xxv. 31, תישבנה, Ezek. xxxv. 9. The Vulg. renders שילל *spoliatus;* the LXX ἀνυπόδετος; the Pesh. ܡܫܠܚ, by one or other form of which all the Semitic Verss. reproduce יחף at Isa. xx. 2, where LXX has ἀνυπόδετος. The reading of the Targ. in our passage is uncertain: for בשולליא of *a*, Levy would substitute בשׁוּלְלַיָא, "sie gehen wie die Ausgeplünderten nackt einher," but this is merely conjectural; *b* reads בשביא and *r* בשיליא, of which the first looks like a reading belonging to another recension of the Targ., and the second like an emendation of בְּשׁוּלַלְיָא.

There is much uncertainty and vacillation in the manner in which the Verss. deal with תנים and בנות יענה. The comparison of a few passages in which these words occur gives curious results. Isa. xiii. 22, xxxiv. 13, xliii. 20, Job xxx. 29 and Micah i. 8, may be taken as examples. In the rendering of תן the Targ. and the Pesh. are consistent throughout, having respectively ירודא and ܝܪܘܪܐ: Vulg. has *draco* and *siren:* LXX ἐχῖνος, σειρήν and δράκων: Ar. قنفذ, ولد وحش, اوى, بنت اوى, and in our passage, تنين. He exactly represents ἐχῖνος at Isa. xiii. 22 by قنفذ, but at Isa. xxviv. 13 deserts ἐχῖνος for اوى: the σειρῆνες also, which at Job xliii. 20 is represented by بنات اوى, at Job xxx. 29 becomes اولاد الوحوش. The Ar. translator was not sure what animal the LXX meant. The Vulg., too, presents a curious phenomenon: at Isa. xiii. 22, where LXX has ἐχῖνοι, it has *sirenes;* in the other places, including those where LXX has σειρῆνες, it has *dracones*. At Ezek. xxix. 3, both LXX and Vulg. confound תן with תנין, as they have done here, and the Ar. follows the LXX.

בנות יענה is in all these passages reproduced by the Targ., and the Pesh. has it in the form ܒܢܬ ܢܥܡܐ in each case except ours, where it follows the LXX (see below). The Vulg. has *struthio* throughout, LXX στρουθῶν, θυγάτερες στρουθῶν, and in our verse θυγάτερες σειρήνων, where σειρήν means a bird of doleful note.* Its use here as a rendering of בנות יענה, compared with its employment elsewhere for תן, shows how uncertain the LXX were as to the precise meaning of these words, with which they had not been familiar in living speech. One of the most curious results, however, is that seen in the Pesh., which has not followed the LXX in its treatment of תן here, but has followed it in dealing with ב״י, and, consequently, has substantially the same rendering for both, ܢܥܡܐ and ܒܢܬ ܢܥܡܐ.

V. 9. נָגְעָה for נָגַע.

For אנושה LXX have κατεκράτησεν: they seem to have read אָנְשָׁה, 3rd sing. fem. perf.; the Ar. so understood them, and as the vowel letter ו was probably not found in their text we can readily trace their procedure. But their inability to understand this word in other places

---

* Jerome's comments reveal a remarkable error on his part: "Et lugebunt quasi filiae Sirenarum: dulcia enim sunt haereticorum carmina, et suavi voce populos decipientia. Nec potest eorum cantica praeterire nisi qui obturaverit aurem suam, et quasi surdus evaserit." Evidently he is thinking of the sirens of the poets.

renders their judgment on it untrustworthy: at Isa. xvii. 11, כאב אנוש is rendered ὡς πατὴρ ἀνθρώπου, at Jer. xvii. 19 we have ἄνθρωπος, at xvii. 16 ἀνθρώπου, at xxx. 12 ἀνέστησα (from נשא?): at Job xxxiv. 6, Theodotion's rendering is βίαιον, just as Symm. and Theod. have βίαια here. Ryssel is of opinion that the LXX thought of a verb אנש, meaning "to be manly or strong," and urges the analogy of גבר. But there is no real analogy; such a passage as 2 Sam. xii. 15, where וַיֵּאָנַשׁ is translated ἠρρώστησε, shows too plainly how far removed from such a meaning this root is. There is much more to be said for his suggestion that the Vulg. *desperata* came from a confounding of אנושה with נאשה, fem. Niph. partic. of יאש: Jer. ii. 25 and xviii. 12 confirm this.

All the Verss. for מכותיה have the sing. It was hardly possible for such languages as Greek and Latin to put it otherwise. Pesh. may have followed LXX here. At all events it is difficult to believe that the M. T., which is the harder reading, would have been introduced in place of the easier sing., and, on the other hand, the plu. is not contrary to Heb. Grammar.

Between the two ע the ה at the end of נגעה might easily disappear: Pesh. and Targ. have the fem., and Ar.* understood the LXX so, or else followed the Pesh.: it is difficult to believe that there is here a change of subject when nothing indicates what the new subject is, and there certainly is no justification for supplying in thought, with

---

* The Polyg. translator is in error in representing the Ar. as having the plu.

Hitzig, a synonym of מכה such as שבר. The LXX (καὶ ἥψατο) and Pesh. again avoid the asyndeton. They and the Vulg. have the sing. ἕως πύλης, in agreement with the M. T.: the Targ., quite unnecessarily, has the plu.; a city has more gates than one, but it is enough if calamity reaches one of them.

a and *b* of the Targ. insert the frequently used בית before יהודה: it is better omitted, with *r*.

V. 10. For בְּכוֹ read בַּכּוֹ.

בנת אל תגידו. LXX, οἱ ἐν Γὲθ μὴ μεγαλύνεσθε. They either read or corrected to תגדילו: the Hiph. of גדל is not elsewhere used absolutely for μεγαλύνω, the Hithp. being the form employed, but at Ob. 12 its employment with פה comes sufficiently near the absolute use to account for the LXX having thought of it here. The Pesh. has ܬܬܡܣܘܢ, as if from תגילו: Sebök conjectures that ܬܬܡܣܘܢ should be read; the corruption would be very easily made, but Rich, Add. and Eg. all have ܬܬܡܣܘܢ. The LXX and Pesh. may have arisen from a reminiscence of the exultation of the Philistines referred to in the well-known passage, 2 Samuel i. 20, which was doubtless the original of ours: this supposition would account either for תגדילו or תגילו. Ryssel would strike out בנת אל תג׳, believing them to have been a marginal note which called attention to the fact that the ensuing paronomasiae are according to the model of that familiar passage. He urges that they have nothing to do either with the rest of the section or with the circumstances of the time. But we know so little of those circumstances that our arguments *e silentio* have not much force: there is no reason why Micah himself, just as well as an annotator, should not commence his dirge with a quotation from the one which all Israel knew; and if any thing so formal as an indication of the "schema" had been intended, we should have expected the words to be arranged in the precise order of the original passage, אל תגידו בגת—not, as here, 'בגת אל תג. Aq. and Symm. have μὴ ἀναγγείλητε.

בכו אל תבכו. The first point to be firmly grasped is that this clause is in strict parallelism both with the preceding and the following:—

בגת אל תגידו
בכו אל תבכו
בבית לעפרה עפר התפלשתי

This juxtaposition of the clauses leaves little doubt that a town name is involved in בכו, for it is incredible that there should be a play on the similarity between the town name and the verb in each of the enclosing clauses and none in the middle one. The common text of the LXX has οἱ Ἐνακείμ, which can hardly be original in a parallel clause to οἱ ἐν Γὲθ: A, followed by Ar., has "οἱ ἐ- (versu exeunte) ακειμ." Jerome and Codex Leidensis of Eusebius read ἐν Βαχείμ or Ἐμβαχείμ. Jerome's note assists us in discussing this reading:—"Bachim in nostra lingua *planctum* et *fletum* sonat. Denique exceptis Septuaginta omnes κλαυθμὸν, id est, *fletum*, transtulerunt." On this it is to be noted that the text of the LXX which was before Jerome evidently recognised the name of a town in בכו, most likely the town Bochim of Judges ii, 1, 5, and further, that in all probability the other Greek Verss. thought of the same passage, because the LXX there has κλαυθμῶν, almost identical with the κλαυθμὸν here. But it does not seem likely that βαχεὶμ belongs to the original LXX: at Judges ii, 1, 5, as we have seen, βαχεὶμ is not used, but κλαυθμῶν: if βαχεὶμ had stood in our text, the most careless transcriber would hardly have missed the reference to the place mentioned in Judges. A reviser of the LXX would be likely to remember that place, and to improve on the meaningless ἐνακεὶμ by inserting the β. This brings us to the older ἐνακεὶμ.* If the μ is a reduplication of that in the next word μὴ we now have ἐν 'Ακεί, and the town Accho, which the Greeks always reckoned to belong to the Phœnicians, is in Strabo 'Ακή: in MSS. η and ει are constantly interchanged. I believe, therefore, that for the full form בְּעָכּוֹ, for the sake of the paronomasia, בָּכוֹ was employed, and that when the meaning had been lost this was written בְּכוֹ. To the many examples which have been adduced of the loss of ע in the middle of a word, Ryssel objects that the essential part of every one of these words is retained in the contracted form. But he is obliged to give up this point with respect to בִּי for בְעִי, and it may well be doubted whether such words as רוּת for רְעוּת, and מִן, Cod. Sam. at Num. xxxi. 38, for מְעוֹן, are not equally against him. In any case he admits that there was a process at work in the language which tended to the loss of ע in such circumstances, and it is better to acknowledge its operation here than to follow his counsel of despair and

---

* The Ar. here is a literal translation of ἐν 'Ακεὶμ, في اكِم ; at Judges i. 3, for עָכוּ it has عَكَّة; it therefore does not recognise Accho here.

reject this clause as well as the former one. He urges that the other plays on words depend on the meaning, not merely the sound, of the town-name. But the one preceding this does not, and we, at least, have not rejected that. He points out that the other clauses are lengthy, and this short: the first clause is of the same length as this. He says that Micah had a definite geographical situation in view to which the position of Accho does not correspond: but there seems no good reason why in this poetical utterance a Phœnician town on the north should not be the contrast to the Philistine one on the south, and, as Cheyne says, "the choice of the town would be dictated by the love of paronomasia;" to which may be added Hitzig's remark that although Accho seems never to have belonged to the Israelites their territory extended to it, and the neigbouring Carmel was possessed by them.

For אל תבכו, LXX read אל תבנו : נ was substituted for כ; the paronomasia is thus lost and the sense that results is very unsatisfactory. It will be desirable to set down side by side the M. T. and the reading probably adopted by LXX:—

M. T. אל תבכו בבית לעפרה עפר התפלשתי עברי לכם
LXX-text * אל תבנו מבית לעוג * עפר תתפלשו לעונכם

This implies the preference of B, Ar. and Jer. to the text of A; the latter having καταπάσασθαι instead of καταπάσασθε (αι written in mistake for ε), and ὑμῶν after the first γέλωτα as well as after the second, an insertion made intentionally to produce sameness of expression. Jer. translates *derisum* and *derisum vestrum*, showing that he read

---

* Or לעברה and לעברתכם, on which see below.

καταγέλωτα as one word: but this can hardly be correct; in the first clause a possible sense would thus be obtained, but in the second καταγελ. and γῆν could not well stand together as accusatives after καταπας.

With reference to the text given above as that translated by the LXX, Roorda's suggestion that לעברה may have been the word thought of comes much nearer in form. The objection to it is that עברה is used in a considerable number of passages, but that in none of them is there anything approaching to a translation of it by καταγελ. Yet I think Roorda is right here; wrath and derision are not far removed from each other; the change of letters is very slight, and there is a real difficulty in thinking that the greater change to לעג, which is totally dissimilar in sound, could be made twice within a few words. None of the Verss. agree with the LXX in reading מבית.* They read thus because they were compelled to do it if any tolerable sense were to be obtained: they were misled by their reading תבנו; the parallelism is decidedly against them. On the words בבית לעפרה Baer and Delitzsch's note is:—"לא ספיק ה"א לעפרה E 3. adnotat: לית פתח עין, B: ה"א ספיק לא." The Massoretes therefore recognised the Pathach under ע and the Raphe which shows that ה is not suffix. The Pesh., seeing that the name of a town is required, and concluding rightly that Ophrah, on the Philistine border, is meant, takes no account of the ל, and vocalizes עָפְרָה instead of עָפְ: the Targ. and Vulg. go to the other extreme; perceiving the reference to עפר, they

---

* There cannot be much doubt that they are translating מ: the Ar. certainly understood it so.

let go the town-name entirely בְּעָפְרָא 'בב, *in domo pulveris*. The M. T. is better: it keeps the reference both to עפר and to the town. And here comes in the consideration of the ל: it is in its place, indicating the genitive relation, and it is *required* by the alteration of the customary 'עָפָ to 'עָפְ. The בבית of M. T. is supported by LXX and Vulg. The Targ. has בע בבתיא and דיתבין and the Pesh. also has "houses." This arose from their not connecting בית with לע as part of the name of the town.

Hitzig thinks it impossible to account for the Kethib התפלשתי arising out of the Qeri התפלשי: he also supports the Kethib on the ground that it contains a reference to פלשת. But the two forms are so much alike that either of them might be a corruption of the other. And the reference to פלשת is far-fetched. Cheyne prefers the Kethib, but does not state his reasons. Keil maintains that the Qeri originated in a mistake as to the meaning. To me it seems that the imperative in the midst of so many other imperatives is more likely to be correct than the indic. And the Verss. are strongly in favour of this: LXX, Pesh. and Vulg. have 2nd pers. plu. imper., the plu. in the LXX being occasioned by the parallel ἀνακοδομεῖτε. It is also not improbable that the Targ. originally had the imper. Its present representation of בבית לעפרה עפר בבתיא בעפרא יתפלשון בקטמא חפו רישיהון is by התפלשי For רישיהון, the reading of *b*, we must with *a* and *r* read רישיכון: *a* and *r* also omit יתפלשון. If the original text ran 'דיתבין בבתיא דעפרא בק' חפו ר, and יתפלשון was first written in the margin as explanatory of חפו and subsequently was copied into the text, דעפרא, which had previously belonged to דיתבין בב, would be altered into בע׳ to go with יתפ׳, and חפו, which originally was sec. pers. plu. imper. would be regarded as third pers. plu. indic. Ryssel is of opinion that יתפ׳ and בעפרה have crept into the Targ. directly from the Heb. It is to the influence of the Heb. that we owe the former, but לעפרה cannot have been untranslated in the first instance, and the Lond. Polyg. has בעפרא not בעפרה.

V. 11. No alteration.

עברי לכם יושבת שפיר. The LXX, as we have already seen, affix the first words of this verse to the close of v. 10. They have no countenance from the other Verss., and the change that would be needful in the form of the words, as well as the unsatisfactoriness of the result obtained, discredits their procedure. The Targ., which so often turns these collective singulars into plurals, has עברו לכון דיתבין בשפיר, which may be taken as evidence in favour of the M. T. Jerome has "Transite* vobis, habitatio pulchra." The plu. imper. has arisen from the plu. pronoun, just as the Pesh. has turned the pron. into the sing. to agree with its sing. imper. Neither change is necessary; the sing. imper. is sufficiently explained by the noun to which it refers, יוש׳, being sing., and the plu. pron. by the fact that יוש׳ is a collective. As to the ܐܒܡ of the Pesh., it is evidently a mistake arising from a confusion of ܘ and ܟ, although Rich, Add. and Eg. support

---

* The common text of the Vulg., as well as Cod. Amiat., have "Et transite," &c. But neither the M. T. nor the other Verss. have the conjunction, and in two places in the Comm. we have the simple "Transite."

the text. All the Verss. read יושבת שפיר: LXX κατοικοῦσα καλῶς, and Vulg. *habitatio pulchra*, regarding it as
an adjective or adverb; Targ. and Pesh. correctly taking
it as a town-name. Both the latter are incorrectly rendered in the Polyg.; the Targ. by "qui habitatis in pul-
chritudine," which is sufficiently condemned by the fact
that שפיר means *pulcher*, not *pulchritudo*, and the latter
by "Fac tibi ipsi O habitatrix quod bonum est," where
"O hab. quod bonum est" is the translation of a precisely
similar construction to that which in this same verse
is rendered "habitatrix Soanis." It may be added that
Jerome himself looked on "habitatio pulchra" as a name
given to Samaria because of its beauty and fruitfulness.

עריה בשת. The Targ. has a double translation—
גלו־עריא ערטלאין בהתין, where גלו־עריא is, as Geiger
says, assuredly a later addition, עריא being a word which
the Targ. avoids. The two remaining words ער׳ בה
allowance being made for the Targ. use of plu. for sing.,
will thus exactly represent our M. T. The Vulg. has
confusa ignominiâ (in Comm. *confusa es ignominiâ*), as
if from עור "to excite." The remaining two translations
diverge from these, and from each other. LXX end the
first clause where the M. T., Targ., and Vulg. do, κατοικοῦσα καλῶς τὰς πόλεις αὐτῆς (from עָרֶיהָ in place of עֶרְיָה),
except that it omits בשת. In this omission it stands
alone, and not improbably has been led to it by confusion with one of the יושבת, either above or below.
The unsatisfactory sense it obtains and the error in its
treatment of שפיר are decisive against its rendering. The
Pesh. ends the first clause at שפיר, and proceeds as though

the next clause ran עריה יצאה לא בושה* יושבת צען. But it would be a strange threat that the people should go into captivity "stripped, yet not ashamed." Possibly a reminiscence of the "naked and ashamed" of Gen. iii. was in the mind of the translator, and, embarrassed by the somewhat difficult עריה־בשת, he brought out a contrast to the narrative in Genesis. His division of the words would rob the clause of the play on the name which is found in the parallels and is supplied here by the juxta-position of "beauty" on the one hand with "nakedness" on the other.

The only Vers. which has preserved the צאן of M. T. is the Targ. צאנן, thus spelled, does not occur elsewhere, and it is probable that the א was inserted for the purpose of making the word liker to יצא: at Josh. xv. 37 it is צנן. The Vulg. is *in exitu*, but there can be no doubt that this is a translation of the M. T.: in the Comm. Jerome has:—"*Non est egressa quae habitat in Sennan*, quae interpretatur *exitus*, sive ut Symmachus vertit . . . . *habitatio abundans*." Symmachus has εὐθηνοῦσα, from שאנן. And it is most likely that the LXX in like manner confused ש and צ: Jerome and several cusives have Σενναν or Σαιννάν—צנן, Josh. xv. 37, in B is Σεννά, and in A Σεννάμ—but this is a correction made under the influence of the Heb.; the other MSS. have Σενναάρ, from שנער, and the Ar., El-'Irak, follows this. The Pesh. is ܠܒ, and at Josh. xv. 37 it almost certainly had the same word, for the ܠܒ now found there is the easiest of corruptions.

---

* This is better than Seböks לא ידעה, because his suggestion leaves בשת out of sight.

מספד בית האצל יקח מכם עמדתו. So far as the construction is concerned the Pesh. is correct in making מספד the subject of the clause. Each of the other town-names in this verse is preceded by a word in the construct, and the sense obtained by adhering to this order in our passage strongly recommends it. The Vulg. supports the placing of מספד in this clause, although it makes it the object of the verb, "planctum Domus vicina * accipiet ex vobis." LXX agrees with M. T., κόψασθαι οἶκον ἐχόμενον αὐτῆς, which belongs in sense to the preceding clause. In saying this we assume that B κόψασθαι is to be preferred to the κόψασθε of A, and that the latter either arose from αι being mistaken for ε or from an intentional introduction of the imper. in conformity with those already used. The Ar. agrees with B, although Jerome's text is like that of A. The difficulty in believing κόψασθε original is that it can hardly have been got from מספד whereas the infinitive easily might. The unsatisfactoriness of the division adopted by the LXX appears best when we consider that the new clause λήψεται κ.τ.λ. is left in the air without any proper subject: יקח can hardly have the fem. 'צ יושבת as subject, although that is what this translation implies.

בית האצל. The Pesh. is the only Vers. which explicitly recognises the proper noun here, although the Vulg., as we have seen, rests on that. The Targ. is uncertain: the Polyg. gives בית צוּלָאֵי, but Levy says "צֵלָאֵי *m. pl.*

---

* Cod. Amiat. *vicinae* is a transcriber's error. In the Comm. the translation is, "planctum domus Asel"; and Jerome remarks, "domus vicina et ex latere quod interpretatur Asel."

(Gerber) *n. pr.* einer Stadt, Micha i. 11, צלאי Levita."
The ἐχομ. αὐτῆς of LXX is due to the fact that the town was an obscure one. It is nowhere else mentioned, unless אֵצֶל, Zech. xiv. 5, be the same place. In that passage also the varieties of rendering are noticeable ; LXX, Ἰασόδ, Targ. אצל, Vulg. *vicinum*, Pesh. ܐܟܠܒ. It is worth noticing that the ה of האצל is not reproduced either in Targ. or Pesh. Yet the ה is assuredly original. Similar forms occur elsewhere, such as בית הצמק, בית המרכבות. It may have originated here in the recollection of האבל and the mourning for Jacob which took place there, ויספדו שם מספד גדול.

עמדתו is a very difficult ἀπ. λεγ. and has occasioned great perplexity to the translators. The Vulg. has *quae stetit sibimet*, as though it had read עָמְדָה לָהּ, which however cannot have been the case, seeing that there is no trace of such a reading. Jerome must therefore have educed this sense out of our עמדתו. The Targ. has שפר ארעכון, where the ו of the Heb. is turned into כון to make it accord with the signification ascribed by the Targ. to the whole clause. The שפר probably arose from חמדתו * being read instead of עמ': it can hardly be considered adverse to this explanation that מרות in the next verse is also rendered שפר ארעא. The LXX has πληγὴν ὀδύνης, and the Pesh. ܟܐܒܗ̇. The ע of עמדתו was dropped, the ד read as כ, and the suffix, which doubtless was written ה,

---

* Steiner would admit הכמדתו into the text: he says, " Der Sinn : nimmt von euch, nimmt euch weg seine *Annehmlichkeit*, *Lieblichkeit* ist ein völlig angemessener." But how could the *wailing* of Beth-Ezel have *Annehmlichkeit* ?

was regarded as fem. (see below), in accordance with what was believed to be the subject, κατοικοῦσα. Roorda is no doubt right in conjecturing that the original was πληγὴν αὐτῆς, and the ὀδύνης came from the scribe's eye having fallen on this word in the next line. The Pesh., which here depends on the LXX, favours this. In justification of the order we have adopted, the sense thus obtained must be given: "The mourning of Beth-Ezel shall receive from you its standing-ground": Beth-Ezel, the house on the slope, may appear to have an insecure standing-ground, but there is secure standing-ground for the mourning and misery thereof. The paronomasia is thus preserved.

The Targ. stands so entirely alone that some remarks need making on those portions of it which have not yet been referred to. The sense of לא יצאה יוש׳ צ׳ is not unaptly given by מיתבי צ׳. לא יפקון משזבין [*b* has יתבי, *a* and *r* מיתבי]. מספד בית האצל is explained by an imper., and the cause of the weeping עבידו לכון מספד לקח מכם עמ׳. For במרד* על קטילי גבריכון בית צולאי there are two renderings, the shorter one at the end of the verse, ובכן יתנסיב מנכון שפר ארעכון, being probably original, and the longer one, בתי חמדתכון דהויתון אנסין ומקרבין דין לספר דין, being a later explanatory addition from that book of Isaiah with which Micah has so much in common. Cf. the Targ. on Isa. v. 8, וי דמקפין ביתא על ביתא חקל אונסא בחקלתהון מקריבין.

V. 12. חָלָה for הֵחִילָה.
After יושבת ש׳ and יוש׳ צ׳ it would be unaccountable

---

* In *b* במרך, a mistake of transcription; *a* and *r* as above.

if יוֹשׁ׳ מרות were to be separated as Pesh. has separated them, inserting *o* and treating 'מ as 3rd pers. sing. of the verb عَدَى. The similarity of sound misled it; and to this must be added that nothing is now known, probably nothing was known when Pesh. was translated, concerning a town of this name. The other Verss., though supporting the M. T., know nothing of this place: LXX, ὀδύνας; Symmachus, ἡ κατοικία ἡ παραπικραίνουσα; Vulg., *in amaritudinibus*; Targ. (see on v. 11), שפר ארעא.

The force of the two contrasted halves of this verse is destroyed by the τίς ἤρξατο of LXX, where מי is read instead of כי, and for הֵחֵלָה, חָלָה. The Vulg. and Pesh. read our M. T., and translated "*infirmata est;*" so also Aquila, ὅτι ἠρρώστησεν. A much more picturesque rendering is that of the Targ., מסברא, "She looked for good: evil came!" To get this, however, we seem to need the Hiph., not the Kal, of חול, the instances adduced, such as Gen. viii. 10, Judges iii. 25, not justifying our ascribing this sense to the Kal of the verb. If we assume that the vowel letter י was not written, and that the Targ. had the same consonants before it as the LXX, we shall have הֵחִילָה, which will give the excellent sense mentioned above, and will recommend itself also by its likeness to the text translated by the LXX. Theod., too, has ἀναμένουσα, and it is worth noticing that he read רמות, εἰς ὕψος.

Jerome's LXX has the nom. κατοικοῦσα, not the dat. of A and B and the Ar. The dat. is probably original: only from it can a tolerable sense be extracted. There is a little uncertainty respecting Jerome's own translation of

לטוב : the common text and Cod. Amiat. have *in bonum;* the text of the Comm., *in bono;* and the comment itself is "infirmata bono suo." *In bonum* is most likely original, the quite fitting interpretation of this by the Dativus Incommodi might lead a transcriber to write *in bono* in the text.

Targ. and Pesh. have the plu. שערי; A and B of LXX and Jerome's LXX likewise; the Ar. has the sing.; the Vulg. has *portam*. We must adhere to the M. T. It is, of course, true that the י of שערי would easily fall out before the י which begins the next word. But it is equally true that י might be read twice by reduplication. The sing. is more likely to have been altered to plu. than the plu. to sing., because it would seem strange that Jerusalem should be spoken of as though it had only one gate. The parallel passage, v. 9, where LXX, Pesh., and Vulg. all have sing. is in its favour here. LXX, κακὰ for רע, as in other passages, to show that the evil is misfortune, calamity, not moral evil.

In the Targ. the title יוש׳ מ׳ is placed emphatically at the beginning of the verse as a parallel to מס׳ לטב : "For she who dwelt on the pleasant place of the earth and looked for good." To the simple "looked for good" is added one of those paraphrases which the Targumists introduced in the course of their reading, "and she looked to be turned again to the Law." To connect the two clauses the rhetorical question is now inserted, "What will ye do? for," &c. This question would not have been felt necessary if the explanatory ומס׳ למתב וגו׳ had not been interpolated.

The connection of יר׳ לש׳ with next verse in Pesh. is treated of below.

V. 13. No alteration.

The abrupt opening of this verse by the word רתם led the Pesh. to begin with לש׳ יר׳, and taking the ה of המר׳ as final letter of רתם it obtained a 3rd pers. fem. indic. agreeing with the verbs which have preceded. The ל of לש׳ it represents by ܒܐ, just as ל in this same verse appears as על in the Targ. The LXX for רתם המרכבה has ψόφος ἁρμάτων: the המר׳, like רכש, which are collectives, being treated as plu. They cannot have read רתם: Ryssel suggests רקע, which at Ezek. vi. 11 is rendered ψοφέω, but this is too unlike in sound and not near enough in form; they are more likely to have thought of המון. The Vulg. *Tumultus* is from the LXX. The Targ., like the Pesh., supports the M. T.: it has the plu. imper. in accordance with its general procedure in this passage, and the plu. for the collective noun, טקיסו רתיכיא.

In rendering רכש by ἱππευόντων the LXX have, in substance, followed their usual course with this word. In Gen. xiv. they read רכש three times, and used ἡ ἵππος: at Esth. viii. 14 they used οἱ ἱππεῖς. For לרכש here they read ורכש: they were led to this by their knowledge that רכש elsewhere is an animal for riding, not for driving. The Targ. got over the difficulty by making two distinct clauses, ט׳רת׳ רמו על רכשא. It, the Pesh., and the Vulg. (*stuporis*, taking ל as sign of genitive), all read ל. In using the word *stuporis*, Jerome must have been thinking of some other word, probably רעש: he seems to have been uncertain how to treat it for in the Comm. he contents himself with copying the LXX:—"Veniet ... et ad te quadriga et equites." The LXX and Pesh. division of the verse, putting a full stop after ἱππευόντων, is incorrect: לכיש belongs to the same clause as לרכש. The common Vulg. text has *habitanti Lachis*, Cod. Amiat. *habitant in*, Comm. *habitantis*: the first is best, it explains the others; none of the parallels have the plural *habitant*, and where they have *habitat*, *quae* precedes; it is unlikely that four genitives would stand together. Cod. Amiat. is also in error when it omits *in te*: the scribe's eye fell on the following *inve*, and thus the *in te* were lost.

There is no disconformity to the M. T. of the rest of the verse in the Verss. The Polyg. is wrong in rendering the Ar. "Origo peccati habitatricis Lachis tribuenda est filiae Sionis": it should have been identical with the rendering of the Pesh.:—"Habitatrix Lachis origo peccati est filiae Sionis." ساكنة is obviously the subject, and to it, not to the masc. راس, does the fem. pronoun هي refer. Ar. follows A in the erroneous αὐτῆς instead of αὕτη, but not in having the article before ἀσέβειαι. As usual, the Targ. has the plu. instead of the sing. חטאת; for פשעי the persons who are guilty of these, מרודי; for 'בת צ, כנשתא צ'.

V. 14. No alteration.

The Targ. for שלוחים is קורבנין, and the Syr. ܡܫܕܪܘܬܐ; the latter being admirably rendered in the Polyg. *mis-*

sam facies : LXX and Vulg. punctuated שְׁלוּחִים, and took it as meaning *emissarii*: if this had been the correct punctuation נתן is not the verb we should have expected; in fact, to express this idea we should have looked for one of the customary phrases שלח צירים or שלח מלכים. Aq., Symm. and Theod. had δῶρα. The sense conveyed by the M. T. is perfectly appropriate; תתני של meaning, as Gesenius puts it, "Dimisit, alienavit, cessit possessione," and this being put in contrast with מ׳ גת. In this way also the על (which LXX, ἕως, must have read עד) is explained: in the ת׳ ש׳ is involved the pronouncing, as it were, of a sentence upon Moresheth-Gath. The Moresheth must be retained as part of the proper name, notwithstanding the agreement of the Verss. in turning it otherwise: amongst them the Targ. stands alone in regarding it as a collective like יושבת and rendering it by the plu. מחסיני; it was led to this by its wrong interpretation of שלוחים. The δώσει of B, Jer. and Ar., is clearly original: δώσεις of A is a correction to accord with Heb. But the M. T. is right: the י of תתני was most likely not written, but the second pers. is quite in place: Targ. and Pesh. have it.

The LXX attaches בתי אכ׳ to the first clause, its οἴκους ματαίους (Aq. ψεύδους or ψεύσματος, Symm. Ἀχζίβ, Theod. ἐξ ἀνάγκης)· being governed by δώσει which now takes a somewhat different signification from that which it has when governing ἐξαποστελλομένους :—" he will send messengers . . . . he will cause houses to be &c." The other Verss. keep בתי אכ׳ in their proper clause : the Targ. having בתי אכזיב יתמסרון לעממיא בחובין די פלחו בהון

לטעותא מלכי יש׳, where לאכ׳ למלי׳ יש׳ seems to be represented first by the idea that the houses which they hoped to hold are handed over to others, and, secondly, by the word טעותא, which signalises the idols as vain and misleading: the Pesh. having the same word for אכזב as for אכזיב. None of the others resemble the Pesh. in this particular, but they all, except the Targ., treat אכזיב as if it were not a proper name. B εἰς κενὸν ἐγένοντο, and A εἰς κενὰ ἐγένετο, both come from εἰς κενὰ ἐγένοντο; similarities of sound led to this being written κενὰ ἐγένε. on the one hand, and κενὸν ἐγένον. on the other. For ματαίους the Ar. has القوية, which the Polyg. renders *potentes*: it may be doubted whether the Ar. wrote thus; if he did, it can only have been because he thought a word was needed which should contrast with κενὰ, and yet wanted to retain a reference to قو, *desertum*.

V. 15. No alteration.

The LXX connects this with the former clause of v. 14, δώσει ἐξαπ. ἕως κλ. Γέθ .... ἕως τοὺς κληρονόμους ἀγάγωσι. In this it stands alone, and against it is the consideration that it takes הירש out of the clause which has in it מרשה. With this division falls also the עַד: all the rest read עֹד;* we can easily understand how it came to be wrongly pointed; it is written *defective*, and a עַד immediately follows and by the LXX was also read for עַל, just before. In a passage where the LXX appear to have been somewhat at a loss, we cannot forsake the אבי of

---

* Symm. has ἔτι.

M. T. and the remaining Verss., Symm. and Theod. included, in favour of the pl. ἀγάγωσι.* The fact that the word is written *defective* (as is the case also at 1 Kings xxi. 29 in the immediate vicinity of the story of the other Micah), is in its favour, and the LXX were misled by the sense they ascribed to the passage as a whole. The pl. κληρονόμους does not imply a Heb. plu.: הירש was regarded as a collective; moreover, the plu. noun was needed after ἀγάγωσι, because the people would not bring a single person as heir: מחסנין of the Targ. does not support the LXX plu., for it comes from the previous verse: Aq. and Symm. have κληρονόμον. Κατοικοῦσα Λαχεὶς κληρονομία is evidently erroneous: instead of translating לָךְ, the LXX has joined these letters to the beginning of the next word, which was probably written ישבת, and has thus obtained לכיש; the analogy of the other verses where town-names are used has, however, compelled it to put in יושבת. But the proper name wanted is not Lachish, but Mareshah, to correspond to הירש. Before the Lachish thus obtained the customary κατοικοῦσα was now placed, and the בת, the remaining part of ישבת, was taken to belong to the line next below where it is translated τῆς θυγατρὸς.

What has already been said will make it apparent that the final clause cannot begin with מרשה, but must commence at עד. It is almost certain that the M. T. of these words is correct, although the Verss. are not agreed either

---

* Jerome's translation of, and comments on, the LXX show that his text had the sing. But this was a correction which may have been introduced under the influence of Symm., who has ἔτι κληρονόμον ἄξω.

in the reading or the division of them. The Vulg. follows M. T. The Pesh. read עולם for עדלם, unless, as Roorda thinks, this is an error of transcription in the Syr. I do not myself think it is such an error, because the choice of the verb ܢܓܠܐ as the rendering of יבוא appears to be the result of the presence of עולם, it being felt impossible to make sense of עד עולם יבוא unless a meaning somewhat different from the ordinary one were given to יבוא. It was so easy to mistake ד for ו that we need not hesitate to ascribe this mistake to the translator here. The common text of the LXX has κληρονομία ἕως Ὀδολλὰμ ἥξει, ἡ δόξα τῆς θυγ. Ἰσ. "Ed. rom." has ἕως Ὀδ. κ.τ.λ., making ἡ δόξα the subject. Symm. ἕως Ὀδολλὰμ ἥξει τῆς δόξης Ἰσ., where τῆς δόξης is in apposition with Ὀδολλάμ. Theod. (in Field), κατοικοῦσα Λαχεὶς κληρονομία· ἕως Ὀδολλὰμ ἥξει ἡ δόξα—τῆς θυγάτρος Ἰσ. The Targ. makes two clauses, עד עד׳ יסקון ויעלון בתחום ארעא דיש׳, where the second verb originated in the having mistaken גבול for כבוד [At Am. i. 13, גבולם is rendered תחומיהון]. The Polyg. has mistranslated the Ar.: instead of "O habitatrix Lachis quae es haereditas, ad Odollam veniet gloria filiae Israelis," it should be as the Greek from which it comes, "O habitatrix Lachis. Haereditas ad O.v.g.f.I." Three times in the Comm. we find *usque Odollam*: this might easily be written *usque Adollam*, as in Cod. Amiat.; then, to obtain the restoration of the O, *usque ad Odollam*, as in commom text. After עדלם Ryssel would add עַד עָלָם in order to obtain the play on words which characterizes the passage as a whole. But this is not necessary. There is a sufficiently striking

contrast in the meaning of the words as they now stand :—
"The glory," i.e. the nobles, (Isa. v. 13), "of Israel shall be driven to the outlaw-state, taking refuge in the cave which aforetime sheltered David and his men." "Vortrefflich erklärt *Movers* (die Chronik u.s.w. S. 136) unsere Stelle durch die 1 Chron. iv. 38-40 (vgl. v. 41) angeführte Thatsache, dass zur Zeit Hiskia's mehrere Stammhaüpter der Simeoniten in den Süden Juda's geflohen sind." *Hitzig.*

V. 16. No alteration.

Jerome's LXX is represented by him to have begun this verse with the words which our editions end the last with :—"Hoc quod dictum est a Septuaginta, *gloria filiae Israel,* addentibus *filiae,* Hebraei in fine superioris capituli legunt." No doubt it seemed very suitable as subject to the fem. verbs which follow.

For גוי the Targ. probably read רָנִּי: it uses רמא, in the sense of "lift up thy voice," as Prov. viii. 1, where it has the full expression תרמי קלה; it expected an additional sign of mourning, not a continuation of one already mentioned. It endeavours also to explain הרחבי קרחתך הא כנשרא דנתרו גנפוהי כן אנסי מרט ברישך by כנשר על בניך.

Χηρεία, B, or Χιρία, A, can hardly be original. Jer. and the Ar. read a word which was either derived from or connected with ξυρέω. Possibly the spoken dialect may have had some such word as ξυρεία which was used here in place of the ξύρησις found at Isa. xxii. 12: not being an ordinary literary form this would be altered by transcribers, and our present readings might easily result. There can never have been any mistake as to the meaning of the Heb. word here. Aq. and Symm. have φαλάκρωσιν, and Field says that some MSS. of the LXX have ξύρησίν.

CHAPTER II.

V. 1. No alteration.

הוֹי is not necessarily followed by a preposition (see Isa. i. 14, 1 Kings xiii. 30): there is therefore no need to read היו with the LXX: Aq. and Symm. have οὐαί. The Vulg. stands alone in rendering the partic. by the sec. pers., *cogitatis*; immediately after it is compelled to use the 3rd pers. *faciunt*. Κακά is employed for the sing. רע, as at i. 12. For חשבי־און the Targ. has two renderings which, no doubt, were once alternative but now stand together—למינס and למעבד דביש. The asyndeton באור הבקר is much more forcible than the construction with the copulative conjunction adopted by the LXX, and the conjunctions found in the Targ. and the Pesh. of this verse arise simply from their general method of translating it. The suffix pron. in יעשוה is omitted by the Targ., is treated as a plu. in the LXX because of the plurals to which it refers, and in the Pesh. is explained by "that which they devised."

כי יש־לאל ידם. The Verss. fall into two classes. To the first belong the Targ., Aq., Symm. and Theod., which have respectively ארי אית חילא בידיהון, ὅτι ἰσχυρὸν χεὶρ αὐτοῦ, ὅτι ἴσχυεν ἡ χεὶρ αὐτῶν, διότι ἔχουσιν ἰσχὺν τὴν χεῖρα αὐτῶν. The remaining Verss. form the second class. The Vulg. has *quoniam contra Deum est manus eorum.*

The Pesh. has *et attollunt manus suas ad Deum*, the *et* (which ought not to have been omitted in the Polyg.) being chosen as bringing out the sense of כי, not as implying ו. The *attollunt* arose from the eye of the translator having fallen on ונשאו below. The same mistake accounts for ἦραν of the LXX, but in this translation οὐκ was inserted, partly from לאל, and partly because the rendering διότι ἦραν κ.τ.λ. was felt not to furnish a reason for that which it seems to be adduced in explanation of. The exact rendering of כי has made the difference between the LXX and Pesh. here. There can be no doubt of the correctness of the M. T.: the same phrase occurs Gen. xxxi. 29, its equivalent היה לאל יד, Prov. iii. 27, its negative אין לאל יד, Deut. xxviii. 32, Neh. v. 5. And I think there can be no doubt as to the correctness of the translation given by the Targ. Few persons will be satisfied with Geiger's attempt to show that אל ידי means "the god of my hand": such a phrase in Micah would be out of harmony with the whole tenor of his thought. The same objection would not apply to Kuenen's, "because their might is their god." But the negatives, Deut. xxviii. 32, Neh. v. 5, are strong evidence against this.

V. 2. For ואיש read איש.

Baer and Delitzsch's note is: "איש sine Vav. copul. in Soncin. Venet. 1518. 1521. Lombros. Pisana aliis. Ita B E 1 2 3 et plerique codd.. (36 Kennicotiani, 24 Bernardi de Rossi) neque aliter legerunt translatores veteres. Etiam Kimchi testatur copulam abesse." This is substantially correct but needs a slight qualification with regard to the trans. vett. The Vulg., A and other MSS * of the LXX, with the Ar., *a* and *b* of the Targ. omit: but *r* of the Targ. and B of the LXX have the copula, and the Pesh. leaves out ואיש entirely. ו found its way into the text through the reduplication of the ו which ends the preceding word.

וחמדו שדות וגזלו ובתים ונשאו. The Targ. exactly reproduces this, except that it has the somewhat stronger אנס for נשא. The Vulg. also differs only in omitting ו before נשאו. The Pesh. rests on the same text, its ܟܒ̈ܬܐ . . . . ܢܣܒܝܢ being its way of treating the two verbs ונשאו and וגזלו. The LXX is καὶ ἐπεθύμουν ἀγροὺς, καὶ διήρπαζον ὀρφανοὺς†, καὶ οἴκους κατεδυνάστευον. It is not easy to decide whether they had יתמים in their text or no. On the one hand it may have dropped out before the not dissimilarly formed ובתים: on the other hand they may have thought that an object needed supplying after the verb, or else may have misread ובתים into יְתֹמִים. Against the first supposition is the concurring testimony of the other Verss., as well as the fact that if the object had stood after וגזלו the order of the next words would most probably have been reversed: we should not have had three instances of verb followed by object and one of object followed by verb: LXX itself, and best text ‡ of Vulg., testify to the order we actually have,

---

* "Copula deest in III., XII., 22, 26, 36, aliis et Hieron."—*Field*.

† Field marks ὀρφ. as to be deleted: "Ο' καὶ διήρπαζον—ὀρφανούς."

‡ Common text is *rapuerunt domos*, but Cod. Amiat. and Comm. have *domos rapuerunt*.

though the latter, under the influence probably of the former,* omits the copulative conjunction before the verb. On the other hand the LXX can scarcely have read ינמים for ובתים seeing that they translate the latter word immediately. On the whole, therefore, we must conclude that they were not satisfied with the somewhat peculiar collocation of words in the text, and, failing to see that גזל here is the carrying of the חמד into act and that the word בתים is object to חמד also, leaving ונשאו in precisely the same position as וגזלו, they supplied what they deemed the most likely object, that found in Job xxiv. 9. Treating the passage in this way they were compelled to leave the ו of the verb untranslated.

ובתים ונשאו ועשקו גבר. LXX, καὶ οἴκους κατεδυνάστευον καὶ διήρπαζον ἄνδρα. It is perfectly clear that the verbs are out of place: καταδυναστεύω is the translation of עשק, not of נשא. Admitting the suggestion that נשא might be connected with נשיא, and thus come to mean "to act as ruler over," it remains true that this does not seem ever to have been the case. But עשק is not unfrequently so rendered, and that in the Prophets (see Jer. vii. 6, l. 33, Hosea v. 11, Amos iv. 1, Zech. vii. 10). Elsewhere it is very variously given, ἀδικέω, ἀποστερέω, ἐκπιέζω, παροξύνω, and once, Lev. xix. 13, ἁρπάω. Moreover, in three places where the verbs עשק and גזל occur together, the latter is rendered διαρπάζω; and seeing that διαρπ. has just been used for גזל the conclusion

---

* The Comm. show that Jerome read the Heb. as we do:—"Et domos subauditur, concupierunt; et quas concupierant, diripuerunt."

is inevitable that they read וגזלי here again in place of
ונשאו, rendering it by καὶ διήρπ., and עשק by καταδυ.
When we further note that καταδ. goes better with ἄνδρα
and διήρπ. with οἴκους, we shall also conclude that the
derangement has been in the Greek rather than in the
Heb.

None of the Verss. distinguish between גבר and איש.
The Pesh., for "a man and his house, a man and his
heritage," has "a man in his house and in his heritage"
(*in* is better here than the *propter* of Polyg.). The Vulg.
calumniabantur would seem to be hardly a strong enough
rendering for עשק; yet it is quite common in this Vers.
In the Comm. at Jer. vii. 6, Jerome shows his sense of
its inexactness :—" Non feceritis calumniam (sive non op-
presseritis)."

V. 3. No alteration.

The LXX ὀρθοὶ ἐξαίφνης, or as in A, ὄρθροι ἐξ., is
a double translation of רומה. In some MS. ὄρθροι was
written by mistake: a transcriber corrected this, but put
ὄρθροι in the marg. For this marginal ὄρθροι, ἐξαίφνης
was substituted, and subsequently the latter word found
its way into the text; the uncertainty of its position being
still evident, both in the Ar., which puts it in the very
last place in the verse, and in Jer., who would attach it to
the first clause: his words are, " ἐξαίφνης, id est, *subito*,
in Hebraicis voluminibus non habetur, et tamen potest
cum praesenti loco ita congruere, ut dicamus: propterea
haec dicit Dominus: ecce ego cogito super tribum istam
mala subito." As regards the spelling, which should be

ὄρθριοι, the blunder is not at all an uncommon one. A curiously similar instance is noticed by Hatch, p. 26, "ὁροθετεῖν (many MSS. ὁριοθετεῖν)." The Targ. and Pesh., בקומה זקופה and ܟܣܥܟܠܐ ܦܥܚܝܠܐ ܐܚܠܐ are obviously related to each other. The Pesh. alone has "Lord *God.*" In its rendering of משפחה it exactly follows the Heb., whereas the Targ. limits the extent of the curse,* על עם דרא הדין. The Polyg. should not have rendered the Pesh. by *generationem istam* as though it were identical in meaning with the Targ. At Zech. xii. 13, it renders the same Syriac word *familia.*

V. 4. For נָהָה נְהִי נִהְיָה אָמַר read נָהָה נְהִי לֵאמֹר; for יָמִיר read יָמַד; for לִי read לוֹ.

The passives ληφθήσεται and *sumetur* of LXX and Vulg. do not imply that they read a passive: this is their perfectly legitimate way of treating the impersonal active.

נהה נהי נהיה. If all these words were to be retained in the text one of two accounts would have to be given of them. First, with Gesenius, Fuerst, Hitzig, Cheyne and others, נהיה might be regarded as Niph. of היה. In this way a word-play with נהה is supposed to be obtained. But the effect is rather that of an ambiguity than of a word-play; so much so that all the Verss. missed it. And that ambiguity might so easily have been avoided by אמר נהיה being used instead of נהיה אמר. Besides which, although such an arrangement as "'It is done,'

---

* So *a* and *r*: *b* has not the עם.

they shall say," is not without example in Heb. writers, it is not common: one would rather expect it in Latin or English. Cheyne's plu. has no support in the Verss. except the Vulg. *dicentium*. The second account of the matter makes נהיה a noun from נהי, like לויה from לוי. But *lamentatur lamentationem lamentationis* does not recommend itself, and the reasons urged on its behalf are inconclusive. Ryssel adduces שיר השרים as favouring it. But this is no parallel: the plu. השירים makes all the difference. Pusey says: "The fem. and masc. together make up a whole, as in Isa. iii. 1; or it might stand as a superlative, as in the English margin." So far as Isa. iii. 1 is concerned, the presence of the copula in משען ומשענה removes this passage to another category, and against Pusey's alternative suggestion the objection to Ryssel's holds good. The Verss., no doubt, looked on נהיה as a noun. The LXX, θρηνήσεται θρῆνος ἐν μέλει, the Vulg. *cantabitur canticum cum suavitate*, the Pesh. ܟܒܓܐ ܢܠܥ ܘܟܠܐ all hang together: the Targ. *באיליא ובעינייא is somewhat different but implies the same text. Yet it can hardly be correct. We are led to the solution of the difficulty by observing that with the exception of the Targ., which smoothed away all roughness by the rendering cited above, none of the Verss. were satisfied with the אמר of the M. T.: the Pesh. prefixes ܘ, the LXX has λέγων, the Vulg. *dicentium*. These phenomena are best explained by the supposition that the original reading was וְנָהָה נְהִי לֵאמֹר. By mistake the נהי was written

---

* So *r*: *a* and *b*, ואלא ובעניתיה is evidently an error.

twice, and the indistinct ל of לאמר was read as ה and attached to the second נהי.*

The only departure from the M. T. of the next words is the Pesh. " Praedo nos diripiet," for נשדנו שדוד. The שדוד has obviously been written *defective*, and the נ has been misread as י. The views taken of חלק עמי ימיר fall into two classes. The Targ. and the Vulg. depend directly on the M. T., except that for the impersonal active they substitute the passive מחולקהון דעמי מעדן להון, " pars populi mei commutata est." The LXX and Pesh. read יָמַד, and it is interesting to note that at Ezek. xlviii. 14, where the M. T. has ימכר, the LXX again read יָמַד but the Pesh. supports the M. T. In our passage, Steiner, after Ewald, argues forcibly in favour of יָמַד (or the equivalent יְמַדֵּד, parallel to יְחַלֵּק), on the ground that the thought to be expressed is the measuring out of the land preparatory to its division among the enemies. Ἐν σχοινίῳ has been supplied after κατεμετρήθη from the next verse.

The only Vers. which translates לי is the Vulg. The Targ. has the plu. להון, *more suo*, the LXX αὐτὸν, the Pesh. omits entirely. The LXX and Targ. proceed from the correct text: the third pers., referring to עמי, is wanted, and when the first pers. is required, as it is immediately after, it is in the plu. The Targ. and Vulg. read איך ימיש, though they treat it diversely: ממחסנתהון טרדין להון, and " quomodo recedet a me." The LXX,

---

* When this was written I was not aware that Stade, Zeitschrift f. A. T. Wissenschaft, 1886, p. 122, had come to the same conclusion.

καὶ οὐκ ἦν ὁ κωλύων αὐτὸν τοῦ ἀποστρέψαι, is more probably to be referred to ואין מנע לו (see Ps. lxxxiv. 11), than, with Schnurrer and others, to a reading of our text as a question expecting this negative answer: the change in the form of the words is but slight, and such an answer as is here given can hardly be referred to such a question. The Pesh. partly corresponds to the LXX, "nec erit quis agros nostros mensorio fune restituat," but it substitutes, unsupported by any other Vers., בחבל for יחלק, and it runs the two clauses into one, a procedure which is in some sort adopted also by the Vulg., "quomodo recedet a me, cum revertatur, qui regiones nostras dividat." On the words read otherwise than in the M. T. by these two Verss. it may be safely said that they differ too much from each other to inspire any confidence. Those omitted by the Pesh. are too strongly testified to by the LXX itself, as well as by the other Verss.; and the sense obtained in the LXX is not nearly so good as that of the M. T. So far as the division of the words goes the LXX obtain a last clause which is but a feeble tautology, the Vulg. cannot be obtained from any conceivable text, and the Pesh. has already been characterized sufficiently.

לשובב שדינו יחלק. Both in ancient and modern times the reference of the ל has occasioned perplexity. The Targ. omits it; so also the Pesh. The Vulg. has *cum revertatur*, as if ב had stood in place of ל; LXX, as we have seen, attaches the word to the foregoing clause. For διεμερίσθησαν A has διεμετρήθησαν; the Ar. here follows A. Cod. Amiat. has *vestras*, which probably was an alteration made under the influence of the LXX, the common text and most of the MSS. of which have ὑμῶν, an obvious error, from which several Cursives, as well as Jerome's LXX, are free.

Stade's view of this verse calls for special mention. He holds that the order of the words in the M. T. is incorrect and that the rhythm usual in a dirge is to be expected here. His rearrangements and corrections are as follows :—

חֵלֶק עַמִּי יָמֵד בְּחָבֶל
וְאֵין מֵשִׁיב
לְשׁוֹבֵבְנוּ שָׂדֵינוּ יְחַלֵּק
שָׁדוֹד נְשַׁדֻּנוּ

The transposition of שׁ נ׳ would be a great improvement, which we should be glad to find diplomatic corroboration of. The arguments for some of the remaining changes are not conclusive. "Auch wäre zu ימיש, da der Acker bleibt, doch anzugeben, womit er aufhört." To that it might fairly be returned that in a poetical dirge it is not necessary to specify every detail. "Endlich ist לשובב 'dem Abtrünnigen,' unmöglich: so können wohl die Israeliten heissen . . . . nicht aber die Assyrischen Sieger." But it is the representative of the Israelitish people who is speaking, and he would not hesitate to designate the Assyrian thus: besides which, as Hitzig has pointed out, הַבַּת הַשּׁוֹבֵבָה is used for the Ammonites, Jer. xlix. 4; if for them, why not for the Assyrians? "לי ist Dittographie des ל von לשובנו, welches zu לי ausgeschrieben wurde". This is not altogether without plausibility, but לו (see above) is so strongly supported as to make us pause before rejecting it.

V. 5. No alteration.

A and B of LXX, with Jerome's text, divide otherwise than M. T., Targ. and Vulg. :—διὰ τοῦτο οὐκ ἔσται σοι βάλλων σχοινίον ἐν κλήρῳ. ἐν ἐκκ. κυρίου μὴ κλ. κ.τ.λ. This has probably arisen from the apparent impossibility of regarding קהל יהוה as a space within which a cord might be cast, seeing that its regular meaning is that of an assembly. But undue emphasis is thus given to the words ἐν· ἐκκ. κ., and such passages as Josh. xviii. 8, 10, וישלך להם יהושע גורל בשלה לפני יהוה are sufficiently near in sense to that yielded by the M. T. division here to justify its retention. Cod. Amiat. of the Vulg. has *conspectum* instead of *coetu*, a later alteration to avoid the difficulty which has been referred to: the remark in the Comm. leaves no doubt as to what Jer. wrote :—" Quod in fine capituli juxta Hebraicum posuimus: *in coetu Domini* &c.". The Polyg. has translated the Pesh. as though its division coincided with that of the LXX, but there is nothing in the text to prove this, and it is to be noted that the Pesh. in this verse pursues its own course quite independently of the LXX, prefixing ב to חבל as before, and rendering גורל by the plural.

V. 6. For יַטִּיפוּן read נָטוֹף; prefix כִּי to לֹא of last clause: for יִסַּג read יַסֵּג.

אל־תטפו יטיפון. The LXX is always perplexed with הטיף when it occurs in the sense of prophesying: at

Ezek. xxi. 2, 7, they have ἐπίβλεψον, as if from הבּיט; at Amos vii. 16, ὀχλαγωγήσῃς, as if from טפף. It is only in such places as Amos ix. 13, Prov. v. 3, where the literal sense, or at all events one nearer the literal, is found that they correctly give ἀποστάζω. Here they (and the Pesh. substantially agrees with them) have μὴ κλαίετε δάκρυσι. The Vulg. has "ne loquanini loquentes:" the Targ. לא תתנבון נבואה. The four Versions agree in connecting the second and third words closely together*, and in not reading יטיפון as third word. נָטוֹף, the inf. abs. Kal, would be quite in place, and might well be the source of the translations just mentioned. Cheyne would retain יַטִּפוּן:—"*Prattle ye not* . . . . (*thus*) *they prattle.* The prophet takes up their word and flings it back to them sarcastically." Against this is the ambiguity which would be occasioned by taking up their word thus.

לא יטיפו לאלא. The variations in the phrases adopted by the Verss. do not point to any other verb than הטּיף. The Vulg. has *stillabit*, but the remark made in the Comm. shows that this is merely a more literal rendering of the same word as has just been translated *loquemini*: the LXX has δακρυέτωσαν; Aq. σταλάξατε; Symm. ἐπιτιμῶντε, "fort. ἐπιτιμῶντες:"† the Targ. תילפון: the Pesh. repeats the verb it has already used. But the variations in num. and pers. are remarkable: the LXX, like M. T., has third pers. plu.: the Vulg. third pers. sing.: Aq., Symm., Targ., Pesh., second pers. plu., a

---

* So also Aq., μὴ σταλάξατε σταλάξοντες; but not Symm., μὴ ἐπιτιμᾶτε· ἐὰν επιτιμήσητε κ.τ.λ.

† Field.

correction to agree with the foregoing. M. T. and LXX are preferable to the Vulg., which arose from "non still. super istos, non comprehendet confusio" being taken as the speech of the *loquentes*, and *stillabit* accordingly is put in the sing., parallel to *comprehendet*: the text from which this was taken must have been without the vowel letter ו. A (not Ar.) for ἐπὶ τούτοις has ἐπὶ τούτῳ, a blunder in transcription: Aq. has εἰς τούτους, Symm. τούτους.

לֹא יַסַּג כְּלִמּוֹת. The Targ. robs the clause of all suitable sense, ארי לא מקבלין אתכנעו. The מק arose from an error of hearing, יסג and ישא being confounded with each other (קבל is used for ישא, e.g. Ps. xxiv. 5): אתכ might be the rendering either of sing. or plu.: the plu. verb is used, as in the rest of the verse. The Vulg. has *non comprehendet confusio*, from ישיג. לא ישיג כלמות is rendered *comprehendet* Jer. xlii. 6, Zech. i. 6, Ps. lxviii. 25, and כלמות is used Jer. xxix. 40 (rendered *ignominiam* there). LXX has οὐδὲ γὰρ ἀπώσεται ὀνείδη from כי לא יסג כלמות. The Ar. here has been influenced by the Pesh.: it treats כל' as sing. The Pesh. has "Ne assequatur vos opprobrium quod dictum est de d. &c": the *vos* is obviously an insertion in accordance with what was believed to be the sense of the passage; in other respects the same words as the Vulg. had before it seem to be read.* Both in respect to the verb and the noun the LXX is preferable. The noun has been looked on as sing. by Pesh., Ar. and Vulg. because the verb is so: the

---

* Sebök "sie etwa יסיג lies:" but at Jer. xlii. 16, Ps. xl. 13, lxviii. 25 they have the same verb for ישיג.

alteration of the Heb. from יָסַג to יָסֹג is very slight, and the Hiph. is supported by all the Verss. Three of the Verss. seem to require that another word should stand before לֹא; the LXX and Targ. suppose כִּי, the Pesh. has ‎‏וְ‏‎: כִּי would give a good sense, and being so strongly supported should be accepted. It is, however, to be noted that Aq. and Symm. have not γὰρ: the former reads οὐ καταλήψατε ἐντροπάς, the latter οὐ κωλύει καταισχυμμός.

V. 7. For הָאָמוּר read הֶאָמַר: for הַיָּשָׁר הֹלֵךְ read הַיְשָׁרִים הָלְכוּ.

The Pesh. implies הָאָמוּר: the LXX, ὁ λέγων, הָאֹמֵר: the Vulg., dicit, אָמַר; the omission of ה in the Vulg. finds no support in any of the rest. And the mere setting down of the words found in the LXX will show that their method cannot be adopted: οὐδὲ γὰρ ἀπώσεται ὀνείδη ὁ λέγων Οἶκος Ἰακώβ παρώργισε κ.τ.λ. Why should reproaches be put away by him whose declaration it is that they have been deserved? And would הָאֹמֵר have stood thus at the end of the clause? On the other hand הָאָמוּר cannot be correct. Hitzig adduces Lev. xi. 47, and Ps. xxii. 32, as parallel, but in each of these cases a noun, to which the partic. belongs, is found. Steiner, in editing Hitzig, appears to have felt the force of this objection and expresses his preference for the exclamatory הָאָמוּר, "What a speech!" But this is extremely abrupt. Nor can we take הָאָמוּר to mean "the one who is called:" אמר means to name or call, Isa. viii. 12, but the context there removes all ambiguity, and Isa. xlviii. 1, which has also been referred to, is not relevant, for there is no mistaking the meaning of הנקראים בשם ישראל: Micah, moreover, is not in the habit of insinuating that the people he is addressing are not really, but only nominally, members of the house of Jacob. The difficulty is best solved by the pointing הֶאָמַר, "Doth the house of Jacob say, 'Is the spirit, &c.?'" to which the latter part of the verse is a complete answer, or else that which Driver offers (*Expositor*, 1887, p. 263), הֶאָמוֹר, "the infin. absol., lit. *shall one say?*—used with a touch of passion, as Jer. vii. 9, הֲגָנֹב וגו׳ 'Is there stealing, murdering, committing adultery,' &c., or Job xl. 2, הֲרֹב עִם שַׁדַּי יִסּוֹר, 'Shall a caviller contend with the Almighty?'" Driver's method has the advantage of preserving all the consonants of the M. T. Otherwise it reaches much the same result as the one first mentioned. And it is to be remembered that there need be no special anxiety to vindicate an original place for the vowel-letters and that the LXX does not appear to have read the ו before ר. The inf. absol. preceded by the interrogative particle is also a rare construction. And, on the whole, the more direct appeal, "Doth the house of Jacob say," recommends itself by its greater forcefulness as preferable to the less direct, "Shall it be said, O house of Jacob?"

The arrangement found in the Pesh. yields a good sense, though not that which we have seen reason to attribute to the Heb.:—"Ne assequatur vos opprobrium quod dictum est de domo Jacobi:" The Ar. follows the LXX in connecting this first clause with the last words of v. 6, but in order to obtain what it deemed a suitable sense, or perhaps under the influence of the Pesh., it used يقفي, which is too strong to render ἀπώσεται: it departed still further from the LXX in transposing ὁ λέγων and making a quite different sentence:—"Nam qui dicit non perficit opprobrium." The Targ. is הכדין כשר דאמרין דבית יעקב היתקפד מימרא וגו׳, wrongly rendered in Polyg. by "Numquid rectum istud est, dicit domus Jacob? numquid abbreviatum est verbum &c.?" and wrongly rendered in Fuerst's Lexicon by "One may call with justice, &c." As, at Ps. lxxiii. 11, היכדין ידע אל means "How can God know?" so here, "How can that be right which they of the house of Jacob say 'Is the word,' &c.?" The active partic. אמרין is fatal to Fuerst's view: it shows, too, that the Targ., like the LXX, read הָאֹמֵר. Jerome's LXX would seem to have read ἡ λέγουσα, for he renders it *quæ dicit*. The παρώργισε of LXX and ﺍﺟﻜ of Pesh.* imply that הקצר was taken as Hiph. The phrase is one which they do not render aptly in other places; at Zech. xi. 8, for example, they translate תקצר נפשי by βαρυνθήσεται ἡ ψυχή μου, and קצר רוח, at Prov. xiv. 29, by ὀλιγόψυχος. The Targ. and Vulg. are right in taking this as a question.

οὐ ταῦτα τὰ ἐπιτηδεύματα αὐτοῦ ἐστίν: μὴ would be preferable to οὐ, for the question implies surprise. B has μετ' αὐτοῦ, a reduplication of the final letters of ἐπιτηδεύματα. The Ar. seems to have thought of the collective

---

* There is no need to suppose that the Pesh. read some other verb: Sebök quite justly says that as קצר רוח means "to be wrathful," so the Hiph. might be taken to mean "to make wrathful": and the Pesh. here felt the influence of the LXX.

"house of Jacob," and consequently has the plu. pron. ﻞ. The Vulg. has *cogitationes*, as if from מעלה. The Pesh. differs from all the rest in its arrangement :— "quae ad iram concitavit Spiritum Domini hujusmodi facinoribus suis," reading כאלה מע׳ for אם־אלה מע׳.

Either through a mistaken reading or for the sake of parallelism LXX have οἱ λόγοι αὐτοῦ. All the rest have the pron. of the first pers. And this clause is best read as a divine question which answers that asked by the people : God is the speaker in the first clause of the next verse, "my people." The whole clause runs thus in the LXX *:—οὐχ οἱ λόγοι αὐτοῦ εἰσὶ καλοὶ μετ' αὐτοῦ καὶ ὀρθοὶ πεπόρευνται : instead of our M. T. הלא דברי יטיבו עם הישר הלך they must have read הלא דבריו יטיבו עמה ישר הלכו. This helps us to a more satisfactory text than the Massoretic. עם הישר הלך is defended by Hitzig on the ground that Job xxxi. 26 and Ps. xv. 2 are parallels. But the former of these, though it arranges its words in the same order, וירח יקר הלך, has no preposition, and no article before יקר, and the latter, הולך תמים, does not put the words in the same order and will hardly be thought a parallel if the manner in which it is customary to use תמים be remembered. But if we follow the LXX, and hold that ו has dropped out of the text, we shall get הלכו הישר עם, "with him that is upright in his walk," and the question, "Do not my words (my commands, the effect of which ye have

---

* Aq., μήτι οὐ ῥήματά μου ἀγαθύνουσι μετ' αὐτοῦ εὐθέως πορευομένου; Symm., μὴ οὐ λόγοι μου ἀγαθαποιοῦσι τῷ ὀρθῶς ἀναστρεφομένῳ.

been complaining of), do good to him that is upright in his walk?" is equivalent to a declaration that their misfortunes are occasioned by their lack of uprightness, an idea which is elaborated in v. 8. We thus obtain a parallel expression to the not unfrequent ישר דרך, ישר לב, and we see a better reason than the Massoretes themselves recognised for their carefulness to write הלך *defective.* * The LXX καὶ ὀρθ. πεπ., referring to οἱ λόγ. αὐτ., would give an extraordinary sense. The Vulg. shows no perception of difficulty here, but its rendering can only be defended if some such reading as has now been suggested be adopted: *Nonne verba mea bona sunt cum eo qui recte graditur?* The Pesh. stands alone: "*Ecce verba mea profutura sunt*" (*prosunt* would be better), "*rectis qui profecerunt et perfectos se redderunt.*" The plu. is to be accounted for as in LXX: ואתמול of v. 8 is treated as Hithpa. of מלא, just as at Job xvi. 10, the only passage where this form of the verb occurs, יִתְמַלָּאוּן is rendered ܡܶܬܡܰܠܶܐ. It was the striking position of ואתמ׳ at the head of its clause which gave occasion to this. The Targ. also has the plu., *more suo,* and it paraphrases the whole clause: "Nonne omnia verba mea recta erant quæ me adducturum dixeram? Adduxi equidem omnibus in veritate ambulantibus."

V. 8. Write וְאֶת־מוּל as אֶל־מוּל is commonly written: for יְקוֹמֵם read יָקוּם: for אֶרֶד read אַדֶּרֶת: for שׁוּבֵי either שָׁבֵי or שְׁבוּרֵי.

---

* Baer and Delitzsch's note is: "הלך defective in B. E. 1. 2. Neque enim numeratur in undecim plene scribendis librorum propheticorum."

The Targ. alone omits ו at the opening of the verse, possibly because ממול, with which it commences the next clause, has no copula. But it is correct in making עמי dependent on את־מול, though it does this by a paraphrase: "Because of the sins of my people they are handed over to the enemy." As in the beginning of the next verse something is done against "the princes of my people," so here, "even against my people hath he risen up as an enemy," the "he" being indefinite. Hitzig would alter to אל־כול, but this is not indispensable in order to obtain the sense just given, and the testimony of the Verss. is decidedly against it. Nothing in the context would account for the stress that would have to be laid on ואת־מול if it were taken as an adverb of time. The Vulg. has "et e contrario populus meus in adversarium consurrexit."* The LXX is καὶ ἔμπροσθεν ὁ λαός μου εἰς ἔχθραν ἀντέστη: A has ἀντικατέστη, which perhaps is original; being a non-classical form it might easily be altered to ἀντέστη. Jerome's testimony to the text of the LXX is wavering: in the translation he has *inimicitiis restitit*, but in the comments, *in adversarium restitit*. Here again the Pesh. stands alone: "My people, like a thief, rose up against its peace." גנב and איב are confounded together, and this is facilitated by spoliation being described immediately after.

ממול שלמה אדר תפשטון. The Vulg. has "desuper

---

* Jerome's note is interesting: "quia verbum *Mul*, et *contrarium* et *diem hesternum* sonat, Symmachus apertius transtulit ut diceret: Ante unam diem populus meus quasi inimicus restitit."

tunica* pallium sustulistis." *Tunica* is by no means a good rendering: *pallium*, 1 Kings xi. 29, is the correct word; in other places *vestimentum* or *vestis* is employed. The course adopted here arose from the difficulty of distinguishing between אדרת and שלמה. The Targ. is the only other Vers. which in any way recognises שלמה, and it would seem as though it did not clearly understand either this word or the next: "e regione eorum populi stantes possident eos, pecuniam eorum pretiosam ab eis tollunt." Like the rest, excepting Vulg., it joins the verb יקום (see below) to this second clause, or rather, whilst they make the two clauses into one, it puts the verb into its second clause. The LXX is ἀντέστη κατέναντι τῆς εἰρήνης αὐτοῦ τὴν δορὰν αὐτοῦ ἐξέδειραν. Pesh. is the same, except that the verb is second pers. plu. For אדר they most likely read אדרתו: Gen. xxv. 25, the only passage where אדרת is rendered δορά, might seem to be a weak support for this conjecture, seeing that the context explains the use of δορά there; but עורו, the alternative, though more naturally to be thought of, involves more alteration, besides which עור is almost universally rendered δέρμα. There can be little doubt that אדרת should be read instead of אדר: the latter form is nowhere used in the sense of a garment, whereas the former is fairly frequent.†

---

* In the Comm., desuper tunicam.

† Pusey's note is not without force: "The *salmah* is the large enveloping cloak, which was worn loosely over the other dress, and served by night for a covering. *Eder*, translated *robe*, is probably not any one garment, but the remaining dress, the comely, becoming array of the person..... There is no ground to identify it with the well-known אדרת. It is not likely that the common garment

On the other hand the LXX* and Targ. are wrong in reading the 3rd pers. plu., as the parallel in the next verse shows: they were led into the mistake by the ת of 'תפ being dropped after the ת of אדרת just as the M. T. fell into the reverse error of losing the ת of אדרת. There are three important considerations to be adduced against the reading שלמה of the LXX and its division of the clauses. First, rising up as an enemy *against his peace* is a forced and unnatural mode of expression. Secondly, "against his peace" would hardly have been expressed by ממול של. Thirdly, אד is put in a position of unnecessary emphasis at the head of its clause. With regard to the word יקומם, it is very difficult to believe that it and ממול were written together, the letter מ occurring four times in succession. The first מ of ממול has been written by reduplication at the end of the verb. To Ryssel's objection that there need be no doubt, considering the analogy of other verbs, that יקומם could be used intransitively, it is enough to reply that the Kal is used quite commonly in this sense, and the Pil. never.

מעברים בטח שובי מלחמה. LXX has τοῦ ἀφελέσθαι ἐλπίδα†, συντριμμὸν πολέμου, but fails to obtain a sense

---

should have been called, this once, by a different name; nor that the אדרת, a wide, enfolding garment ...... should have been worn together with the שלמה." But on the other hand no passage can be adduced in which אדר has the meaning thus assigned to it, and if אדרת seems on other grounds the more probable word it might almost, if not quite, as well be used in the required sense as אדר.

* Symm. has ἀπὸ ἱματίων ἐνδυμάτων ἐξεδύσατε κ.τ.λ.

† So A, many cursives, Ar., Jer.: B has ἐλπίδας, through a reduplication of the σ of συντριμμὸν.

thus. They took the מע' for Hiph. partic. The Pesh. agrees with the former part of this translation—*ut amoveatis spem ejus*. The Vulg. (following Symm. ἀμερίμνως), and Targ. take בטח in its customary adverbial signification; the former apparently replaces the מ of מעברים by ו, *Et eos qui transibant simpliciter;* the latter ערן בארעהון לרוחצן. For שובי מל' Vulg. has *convertistis in bellum*. The Pesh. has *et redintigretis bellum*; neither of these requires any radical change in the text, although both would come more naturally out of the active than the passive partic. The LXX συντριμμὸν πολ. supposes the reading שְׁבוּרֵי, and the existence of this as an alternative reading is testified to by the Targ., which has blended it with the other, תיבין בהון יתברי קרבא . No doubt שובי מל', meaning "men who are averse from war," is a good parallel to עב' ב', and שבורי מל' would be an unusual phrase. But שוב in the sense of "to turn away from" is almost invariably followed by מן; Isa. lix. 20 is perhaps the solitary exception, and there it is the *act.* partic., שָׁבֵי פשע. The Targ. reads as though it had originally run כתברי קר' and the ת' ב' been inserted afterwards. So that, taken altogether, the evidence is strongly in favour of שבורי, and if it be not adopted שָׁבֵי must be read. If the latter, it would explain the Vulg. and the Pesh.

V. 9. For נְשֵׁי read נְשִׂיאֵי.

The Vulg. and Pesh. differ very slightly from the M. T. The latter, as so often, inserts ס at the beginning of the second clause. They both use the plu. pron. referring to נשי where the Heb. has the sing. referring to עמי. The

LXX (ἡγούμενοι) read נשׂיאי, not נשׁי. The Targ., with the rest, follows the Heb.; כנישׁת being undoubtedly their translation of נשׁי as it frequently is of בת. The sense of the passage is in favour of the LXX; princes are more likely to have luxurious houses than women in general without any qualification; Micah's denunciations are not against the women but against the chiefs. διὰ τοῦτο of A and Ar. at the beginning of the verse is an insertion to mark the connexion of thought. The 3rd pers. passive ἀπορρι- φήσονται is one of those changes of pers. and voice in which the translators readily allowed themselves and is the less remarkable here as they have altered the 2nd into the 3rd pers. in the preceding verse.

מעל עלליה is represented in the LXX by διὰ τὰ πονηρὰ ἐπιτηδεύματα αὐτῶν ἐξώσθησαν, where the ἐξώσθ. is probably supplied from the verb תגרשׁון * in the first clause, the plu. pron., as in Pesh. and Vulg., refers to נשׂיאי, but does not necessarily imply that they *read* the plu., and τὰ πον. ἐπιτ. is probably from על מעלליה.

תקחו הדרי לעולם now becomes a separate sentence in the LXX, ἐγγίσατε ὄρεσιν αἰωνίοις. For תקחו they read נעו †; for הדרי, הררי ‡; the ל would seem to have been

---

* Jonah ii. 5, נגרשׁתי is rendered ἀπῶσμαι. In our passage Jerome read ἐξηρέθησαν, electi sunt; this must have been due to an error in transcription.

† This is preferable to the supposition that the verb was educed from ל, which has been supported by a reference to Hos. viii. 1, אל־חכך שׁפר. To say nothing of the difference between אל and ל, the LXX—and it is their method we are considering—did not get a verb out of the אל there. εἰς κόλπον is their rendering.

‡ A similar mistake at Isa. xlv. 2, where הדורי is rendered ὄρη.

transposed and put before 'הר. The Ar. retains the 3rd pers. plu. indic. which has hitherto prevailed. There is nothing in the sense obtained by these two Verss. to recommend it in preference to the M. T.: if such an injunction were to be given it should come after the imperatives of the next verse. Ezek. xvi. 14, בַּהֲדָרִי אֲשֶׁר־ שַׂמְתִּי עָלַיִךְ, strongly supports our reading here, and it is to be noted that it has the suffix of the first pers. which the Pesh. in our passage, understanding how glory could be taken away from them, but not how God's glory could, has dropped. The procedure of the Targ. on this point deserves attention:—"The congregation of my people ye have cast forth from their luxurious habitation, taking their sons away from them; their glory is removed which they said should remain for ever." The passage is interpreted under the influence of 1 Sam. iv. 22, and instead of the harsh "*My* glory is taken away from them for ever," we have the characteristic softening in favour of Israel, "*Their* glory which they said should endure for ever."

V. 10. For תחבל וחבל read חֶבֶל תְחַבְּלוּ.

It is somewhat strange that the LXX, which has just had ἐγγίσατε, should now have sing. imperatives, ἀνάστηθι* καὶ πορεύου: the sing. σοι which they have supplied led them to read as sing. these words, which no doubt were written minus the vowel letter ו: it is, however, better to retain the pl. of the M. T. in agreement with the remain-

---

* " Οἱ λοιποί· ἀνάστητε."—*Field*.

ing Verss. and in harmony with the sense of the verse as a whole. Pesh. omits the conjunc. before לכו, missing by accident one of the two concurring ו. A has αὕτη ἡ ἀνάπαυσεις, the last word a common misspelling, the ἡ a reduplication of the η in αὕτη: Ar. agrees with B. The Targ. makes the holiness of the land the reason why it will not bear such inhabitants:—" This is not the land of the house of rest *for the wicked*."

The accentuation of טמאה has occasioned some doubt. Baer and Delitzsch's note is: " טָמְאָה Teth cum Kamez Methegato in E 1. 2. F Lombros. Norziana, quae est Abenezrae quoque et Kimchii (in comm. et sub r. עבר׳) lectio. Attamen E 3. scribit טָמְאָה. Ita scriptum Raschi hanc vocem ante se habuisse videtur. Tertiam lectionem E 2. in margine adnotat טָמְאָה ס״א. Sic Venet. 1518. 1521." Baer and Delitzsch accentuate thus, טָמְאָה: Lond. Polyg. and Athias טָמְאָה. The only Vers. which reads the word as a verb is the Targ. בעבור as a conjunction seems always to be used with the imperf., and Ewald, § 337, b, 2, says that when it means " wegen " it can never be used with the perf. On the whole it is best to regard טמ׳ as a noun. The punctuation of the LXX in the Lond. Polyg. and in Tischendorf's edition is undoubtedly wrong, making this clause clumsy and the next too short. Jerome's is better: he renders the LXX, *propter immunditiam consumti estis corruptione;* so also the Ar. The Vulg. is similar, except that it inserts ejus, *propter immunditiam* * *ejus corrumpetur putredine*

---

* Cod. Amiat. *injustitiam*: but Comm. agrees with ordinary text. The *jam* also of Cod. Amiat., in place of *quia*, is a later correction.

F

pessima. The Pesh. treats בעבור as conjunction, and makes the noun טמאה subject of the clause. The Targ. also makes בע׳ conjunction (see below).

תחבל וחבל נמרץ. The Pesh. reproduces this with the solitary addition of the cognate accus. after תחבל. The Vulg. read תְחָבַּל and omitted ו of וחבל. The LXX, תְחָבְּלוּ חֶבֶל. This would seem the right method: it preserves all the letters of the text, it gives a very good sense which is supported by the Vulg., and it entirely does away with that necessity of supplying a noun after the verb which the Pesh. felt. The Targ. confirms this, so far at all events as to bear testimony to a plural, בדיל טמיותה *אתון מחבלין. Out of the final words וחבל נמרץ the Targ. makes a fresh clause ובדיל לסאבותה אתון מסתיען עלה (*a* and *b* בדיל). In this paraphrase נמרץ is thought of as equivalent to תרוצו: אסתייע elsewhere renders התגודד (Jer. v. 7, Micah iv. 14) and פָּרַד (Hos. iv. 14). In a long and highly elaborated Targ. on מרוץ (from רוץ), Eccles. ix. 11, the partic. מִסְתַּיְעִין occurs. The LXX detach נמרץ entirely from this verse: their rendering κατεδιώχθητε οὐδενὸς διώκοντος implies נמרץ לו איש הלך for תרוצו און הלך or תרוצו לא יש הלך: they are unsupported by the other Verss.; they do violence to הלך; καταδιωκέομαι is very rarely, perhaps only Joel ii. 4, used for רוץ, and the changes needful in the text are too great to allow of our following the LXX here.

V. 11. No alteration.

לו איש הלך רוח ושקר כזב. Notwithstanding the

---

* So *a* and *r*; *b* has אנון, evidently a mistake of transcription.

great diversities amongst the Verss. this clause needs no alteration. The Targ. attaches the לו to the foregoing verse, obtaining thus its עלה. The manner in which LXX treat the first words has already been discussed: for רוח ושקר כזב they have πνεῦμα ἔστησε ψεῦδος, where the ו of ושקר is dropped in order to bring ש׳ and רוח close together, and כזב* is loosely translated ἔστησε. The Vulg., "Utinam non essem vir habens spiritum, et mendacium potius loquerer," stands alone: לולא seems to have been read, derived from לו and the א of איש: הלך רוח might fairly be rendered *habens spiritum*, and כזב, the 3rd pers., be taken to correspond to איש. The Pesh. does not directly render לו, but may still have considered it involved in the translation, "A man who walks in the spirit of lying and of falsehood": nothing calls for remark here save that the ו is transposed. The Targ., "Because they have gone astray after false prophets who prophesy to them by the spirit of falsehood," throws no light on its reading of the more difficult words. The Heb. text, meaning "If a man walking after wind and falsehood lies, saying," &c. is thoroughly satisfactory.

אטף לך ליין ולשכר. The sense of the passage compels us to adhere to the first pers. here, although the Vulg. is the only Vers. which agrees with the M. T. The LXX and Pesh. have 3rd pers. sing., a fact sufficiently accounted for by their general view of the meaning, together with the similarity of אטף and הטף. The Targ. has the 3rd

---

* It is a word which they are not uniform in their treatment of: Ezek. xiii. 19, they have ἀποφθέγγομαι; Hab. ii. 3, εἰς κένον.

pers. plu. The influence of the LXX on the other Verss. is very marked in this passage: μέθυσμα, its rendering of שכר, is frequently found alternating with σίκερα for שכר; but it might very properly be used in the sense of "intoxication," and, in fact, in one passage is so used, translating שִׁכָּרוֹן, Jer. xiii. 13.* Feeling this the Vulg. has *ebrietas*, and the Pesh. ܪܘܝܘ: the Targ. also has רויו. Curiously enough the Ar., having the same word as the Heb., uses it here, instead of translating the LXX. Cod. Amiat. of the Vulg. has *in vino . . . . in ebrietate*: the Comm. agrees with the ordinary text, *in vinum . . . . in ebrietatem*: the ablatives are probably a correction for the purpose of obtaining what might appear a better sense. The Pesh. found it difficult to understand the ל and therefore in both cases neglected it.

והיה מטיף העם הזה. The correspondence with the foregoing vindicates the correctness of this, and the variations from it on the part of the translators arose, most probably, from there being no preposition before העם. The LXX would require מנטף instead of מטיף, from the rarely used noun נטף: the Pesh. follows LXX, and makes the fem. ܪܘܝܘ subject of the clause. The Vulg. makes העם הזה an apposition to the subject involved in היה; its "et erit super quem † stillatur populus iste" being explained by Jerome to mean "populus iste meas suscipiet pluvias, hoc est, vult, non vult, sustinere habet quae dico." The Targ., as given in the Lond. Polyg., is "And it shall

---

* Liddell and Scott have missed this: they only give "μέθυσμα, ατος τό, an intoxicating drink, LXX, 1 Regg. i. 15."

† The Comm. has *quae*.

come to pass that as they have taught to wander after prophets of falsehood, so shall they depart to a land of falsehood, even the people of this generation." This would be a treatment of העם הזה similar to that which we have seen in Jer., and an elaborate development of the meaning ascribed to מטיף. But for דאליפו, *r* has דאיליפו: *r*, however, need not be implicitly followed; the Pael is found in the former clause, and gives a good sense here.* More is to be said for שקריא of *r* in place of the last שקרא: it would leave עמ דרא הדין a parallel to על דרא הדין of v. 3, and the rendering would then be " so shall the liars go forth to a land with this generation." But the sense thus obtained is harsh, and the position of שקריא in the clause peculiar, so that here also the text of *a* and *b* may fairly be adhered to.

V. 12. For צָרָה read בְּצָרָה: possibly שְׁבִיתוֹ should stand before כְּצֹאן.

אסף אאסף יעקב כלך. Pesh. and Vulg. agree with M. T. The Targ. has a double translation of the first word, in the first instance rendering it בסופא, as if from סוף, and then, like M. T., כנשא אכנשכון: *r* has כולהון, *a* and *b* כולכן; it is difficult to say which was original; the 3rd pers. may have been used as in I, 2, and altered to the 2nd for the sake of closer conformity to the Heb., or the reverse alteration may have taken place under the influence of the LXX. LXX has συναγόμενος συναχθσετήαι Ἰακὼβ σὺν πᾶσιν; the συναχθήσεται being probably used not as

---

* If it be adhered to, the Polyg. translation "didicere" is wrong.

depending on a different text, but for the sake of variety. The כלך also is represented by σὺν πᾶσιν, the preposition σὺν being employed because it forms part of the compound verb. The Ar. takes a somewhat independent course:— "Congregem Jacobum et quidem congregetur cum omnibus." In the next clause the Pesh. retains the direct address:—"*Et* omnino recipiam vos† simul, reliquiae Israelis." The Targ. does the same, though with a slight difference, קרבא אקריב גלותכון שארא דישראל כחדא: both of them attaching יחד to this clause (see below). LXX and Vulg. render שארית by plu., τοὺς καταλοίπους, *reliquias*. A (not Ar.) has τοῦ λαοῦ τούτου for τοῦ Ἰσ., by a copyist's mistake, his eye passing on from the λ of Ἰσ., and λαοῦ τούτου being made of λεπιτοαυτο. The Ar., here again, is influenced by Pesh. in joining יחד to this clause. In other passages יחד is found either at the beginning or the end of the clause to which it belongs; the former, Ps. xlix. 3—the latter, Isa. xlii. 14. In this place the arrangement adopted by the Semitic Verss. seems best: יחד at the end of this clause corresponds to כלך at the end of the first one, and each of the three principal clauses begins with a verb.

אשימנו כצאן בצרה. The LXX, which begins this part of the sentence with יחד, divides differently from the other Verss.; ἐπὶ τὸ αὐτὸ θήσομαι τὴν ἀποστροφὴν αὐτοῦ (αὐτῶν of A and Ar. a correction to agree with καταλοίπους),

---

* Et, inserted, as frequently.

† The pronoun is sing., but can hardly be translated save by the plu. here.

ὡς π. ἐν θ., ὡς π. ἐν μ. κ. αὐτ. ἐξαλ. κ.τ.λ.* No other Vers. supports τὴν ἀπ. αὐτοῦ, which the LXX may have put in place of the pronoun owing to their having begun this clause erroneously with ἐπὶ τὸ αὐτὸ, and being then dissatisfied with the bare θήσομαι αὐτόν. It is a little curious, however, that the Targ. has supplied a similar expression גלותכון in the foregoing clause, and this gives rise to the suspicion that the text was uncertain in very early times, and that there may have been a various reading שְׁבִיתוֹ or שבותו †, which the Targ. has wrongly placed in the former clause and the LXX rightly in this. Such a word would correspond better with שׁ יֵשׁ of the former clause than the suffix pron. does. The Targ., as usual, has the plu. suffix: the rest have the sing. בצרה, LXX ἐν θλίψει, Pesh. ܒܐܘܠܨܢܐ ‡. Vulg. *in ovili*, Targ. בנו חוטרא—בנו for ב to produce conformity with next clause. All the Verss. found here the meaning "a confined place," whether they derived this from צרה or, as Driver thinks, from בצר. In the latter case they must have looked on the word as adv. accus., and consequently have supplied the preposition. But Driver admits that "the word does not occur elsewhere in this sense (or, in fact, at all, except as a prop. n.)," and since such a meaning would be quite in accordance with the etymology of צרה, and if adopted

---

* So the ordinary text runs: but see below.

† Ezek. xvi. 53, ושבתי את שביתהן, καὶ ἀποστρέψω τὰς ἀποστροφὰς αὐτῶν.

‡ ܗܢܐ ܒܐܘܠܨܢܐ is unfortunately rendered *oves astipatas* by the Polyg.: *ad angustum usque locum*, the rendering of ܒܐܘܠܨܐ at Zech. xiv. 5, would much better have brought out the connection with the other Verss.

would leave the ב to correspond with the following בתוך, it seems preferable to read בְּצָרָה. In any case, the proper noun Bozrah is out of place even if that town were "the centre of a pastoral district."

כעדר בתוך הדברו תהימנה מאדם. The Polyg. and Athias have הַדָּבְרוּ: it should be accented with Baer and Delitzsch, הַדְּבְרוּ: "Metheg... adjectum est etiam brevi in penultima ante pausam." Gesen. Baer and Delitzsch have a note:—"תְהִימֶנָה sine Jod ante Nun et id ipsum raphatum optimorum codd. consensu, ita ut sit 3 pl. fem. E 3. exhibet התימֶנָה cum nota תהימינה קרי." E 3. therefore regards the word as 3rd plu. fem. of הים, the נָה being a contraction of יָנָה. The Polyg. agrees with B. and D.'s "opt. codd." Athias has נָּה. Gesenius and Ewald refer this word to the Hiph: it would perhaps be better to regard it as Kal, written *defective* for תהימינה, and partaking of the characteristics of verbs Med. י in that תהי is written instead of תהו. For הדבר ויתהי הדברו תהי Roorda and Ryssel would read; but Ewald, § 290, d,* gives several instances where both article and suffix are used, and most of these seem to be uncorrupt: at 2 Kings xv. 16, where a change should be made, it is the article, not the suffix, which should be omitted: in our passage, also, asyndeta prevail, and none of the Verss. has a trace of the copula before תהי. The Targ. and the LXX omit the article. In other respects

---

* To Ewald's instances, add Josh. vii. 21, viii. 33, which Hitzig mentions.

Targ. and Vulg. agree with M. T., the only point requiring mention being the various readings of the Targ. : *b* has תמן, *a* תהימן, *r* המן, the latter being the frequently occurring contracted partic., and the others having obviously arisen from it.* The Pesh. stands alone; ܟܐܢܐ ܥܠ ܢܦܫܬܗ ܕܟܗܐ.† Misled by the ear, they must have thought of הַטְּמוּנָה in place of תהימנה. The LXX ἐξαλοῦνται probably comes from the familiar המם, "to drive or disturb," the idea being that they were so disturbed as to leap out: other verbs, meaning "to leap forth," are too unlike ours in form to allow of our thinking that there has been a confusion with any of them: התמלט, פָּסַח, רָקַד, דלג are examples.

The Ar., the Polyg. and Jerome's LXX begin a fresh clause with ἐξαλοῦνται, but do not agree as to the point at which it ends, the Polyg. and Ar. extending it to προσώπου αὐτῶν, Jer. ending with this verse. No doubt the former was the connection intended, but it labours under the objection that it would necessitate the reading עַל in place of עלה, and that even then we do not get a suitable preposition to use with פרץ or to turn by διά: at Amos iv. 3, פרץ is employed in this sense, but without a preposition. The division followed in the M. T. gives a perfectly satisfactory meaning. The Ar. لِأَجْلِ for διά is

---

* The note in the sixth vol. of the Lond. Polyg. is: " R " (our *a*) "תְּהִימָן, pro quo male in Venetis תַּמָּן, rectius הָמָן ut in Lex. suo Chald. Buxtorf."

† Sebök suggests that the pointing should be ܘܥܠܝܗ: Rich favours this, having ܘܥܠܝܗ, and Eg. has ܘܥܠܝܗ, the vowels apparently having been inked over by a later hand..

a mark of carelessness; it does not distinguish between δία as followed by the genitive and the accusative respectively.

V. 13. No alteration.

Many codices of the LXX begin the verse with ἀνάβηθι, in agreement with Jerome. There cannot be much doubt that this is a correction in accordance with the Heb.; if it had originally stood in the text it would not easily have been lost. For עלה הפרץ לפניהם the Targ. has a double translation; the first part, יסקון משזבין כד בקדמיתא, giving the result of the fact more literally rendered in the second part, ויסק מלך מדבר ברישיהון.

פרצו ויעברו שער ויצאו בו. It can hardly have been from carelessness that the Ar. does not give any translation of this and the next clause; the words are too numerous for us to suppose that. Probably the rejection was deliberate, founded on the belief that the seeming tautologies of the passage were mistaken repetitions; and this would appear even likelier to one whose original was the Greek, where διῆλθον, ἐξῆλθον, ἐξῆλθεν (the last an error) pursue each other. Cod. Amiat. of the Vulg. has *egredientur,* a correction to accord with Heb. and LXX; *ingredientur* of common text is from a different point of view. The Pesh. alone has 3rd pers. sing. ܢܦܩ for פרצו, the verb thus agreeing with the subject of the previous clause*: having employed this verb it cannot

---

* As Jerome in his exposition, *not his text*, makes it, "dux itineris eorum .... quo iter dividente et praecedente &c."

now have its usual noun ܬܪܥܐ, cognate to שער; hence the more general word ܬܖܥܐ. The Polyg. should not have omitted to translate בה. For פרצו Targ. has ויתבר בעלי דבבא דמעקין ∗להון for ויעברו שער: it has ויכביש כרכין תקיפין: for ויצאו בו, in accordance with its treatment of the last clause, קרוי עממיא יחסנוהון: the final clauses of the verse are almost literally reproduced: ויהי מלכהון מדבר ברישיהון by ויעבר מלכם∗ לפיהם, and ומימרא דיי בסעדהון by ויהוה בראשם. The other Verss. also call for little notice: the LXX has ἐξῆλθεν in place of διῆλθεν, probably an early error of transcription occasioned by ἐξῆλθον going before.

∗ So *r*: the Polyg. has דמעיק and renders "inimicum," a procedure which could hardly have been defended even if the verb had been sing.

CHAPTER III.

V. 1. No alteration.

LXX and Pesh. read ואמר. " Cum superioribus haeret sententia " is Jerome's remark. But the leader described at ii. 13 could not be the speaker here. From v. 9 the LXX and Pesh. get ταῦτα and insert οἴκου before Ἰακώβ. Neither the Vulg. nor the Ar. has a word corresponding to the Heb. נא and LXX δή. For קציני the LXX have οἱ καταλοίποι, by which they have rendered שארית just above. Jer. says of the Greek Verss.: " Pro *reliquis d. Is.*, exceptis Septuaginta *, omnes *duces d. Is.* transtulerunt." Neither here nor at v. 9 can the LXX have had any other than our present reading before them : they educed the meaning καταλ. from קציני, owing to the connection of the noun with the verb קצה. The Pesh. and the Ar. have brought out the force of the question in this verse by their verbs " to be becoming or fitting." *a* and *b* of the Targ. have ית דינא: *r* omits the superfluous ית, which had, no doubt, been added for the sake of greater definiteness.

V. 2. No alteration.

אהבי is rendered ζητοῦντες by the LXX; an example, not of change of metaphors as Hatch † takes it, but of

---

* Field gives ἀρχὴ οἴκου as Aq. and Theodotion's reading, ἡγούμενοι as that of Symm.

† Essays in Bib. Greek, p. 17.

metonymy, the effect being put for the cause: the Ar. translates the LXX, and the Polyg. translator has not done well in rendering the Ar. by *amatores*; he has been influenced by the quite correct use of *amatores* to represent the Pesh. word. The LXX, as usual, renders טוב and רע by plurals: the Targ. uses infinitives, לאטבא and לאבאשא which are less correct than the nouns in the Greek translation; if Micah had wished to express the verbal meaning Heb. infinitives were at his command. A has the article οἱ before μισοῦντες, an attempted correction, not followed by Ar. The Vulg. and Pesh., on the other hand, take pains to mark the *sec.* pers. The LXX has the plu. δέρματα and σάρκας—the plu. suffix in עורם is enough to account for this; the Pesh., in both cases, has the sing.; the Vulg. *pelles ... carnem*. The Targ. explains the figurative language by אנסין נכסי עמא מנהון וממון יקרהון * מנהון נסבין. We should have expected the noun עַמִּי in this verse, and the pronoun referring to it in the next; but there is no authority for correcting thus: possibly it was felt that in this verse the use of the pron. could occasion no ambiguity, and in the next the fuller form of expression might be adopted for the heightening of the effect; possibly also the conjunction of sounds, עור עמי מעליהם was offensive.

V. 3. For שְׁאָר עַמִּי אָכְלוּ read אָכְלוּ עַמִּי שְׁאָר, for כַּאֲשֶׁר read כִּשְׁאָר.

Only the Targ. follows the M. T. strictly in the first

---

* *r* has ואנסין, but the אנסין of *a* and *b* is to be preferred.

clause. The Pesh. and Vulg. omit ו; the LXX, for ואשר read כאשר. This is connected with their way of looking on this verse as protasis to the next, ὃν τρόπον . . . . οὕτως; in order to get this connection they were compelled to mistranslate אז, as appears from such a passage as Prov. ii. 5, where אז does introduce the apodosis, yet is rendered τότε, and the protasis opens, not with כאשר but with אִם: to correspond with כאשר, it would be more natural to have כֵן. The M. T., however, is not satisfactory; it would harmonize perfectly with the next two clauses if it ran ושאר עמי אכלו. The not very common שאר would easily be corrupted into אשר and this would lead to the rearrangement of the whole and the reinsertion of שאר in what seemed a suitable place.

A has ἀπὸ τῶν ὀστέων αὐτῶν for ἀπ' αὐτῶν of B: Ar. follows it. It is probably an error of transcription, the scribe having copied the last words of v. 2. For כאשר LXX read כשאר; a much better parallelism is thus obtained, כשאר בסיר corresponding to כבשר בתוך קלחת. The Targ. felt the difficulty of פרשו being left without a noun as object, and supplied אבריא. Hitzig and Ryssel object that שאר does not contain the comparison, and that this must be expressed in the word which follows כְ. But this necessity is more apparent than real: the mind supplies the full comparison from the verb which has just been used, and the assertion that שאר on the LXX method would be compared with itself can only be met with a direct negative. בְ and בתוך are both rendered by לגו in Targ., both treated as simple בְ by LXX and Pesh., distinguished from each other in Vulg.: it is very fitting that the second clause should have a heightened force given it. For τὰ ὀστέα αὐ. συνέθλασαν of B, A has τ. ὀ. αὐ. συνέκλεισαν. If the original was συνέκλασαν, which is more suitable than συνέθ., this might easily be corrupted into συνέθ. and συνέκλει. The translations made by the Polyg. in this verse are open to much criticism. They use *substantiam* for נכסי, thus obscuring the connection with v. 2, where they have *facultates* for the same word; they omit *eorum* after *ossa* in rendering the Ar.; they turn all the third pers. plu. verbs of Pesh. by 2nd per. plu. Except the Targ., the LXX is the only Vers. which distinguishes between שאר and בשר, using respectively σάρκας and κρέα. The Targ. varies very remarkably in verses 2 and 3:—

| M. T. | עור | שאר | שאר | עור |
| Targ. | נכסי | כמון יקיר | נכסי | מכון יקיר |

They seem to have wished to follow the same order in the two verses. The former part of v. 3 they render as in v. 2, but become more literal in the latter half; after the figurative ואת־עצמתיהם פצחו for ית שארהון מנמרין they have the enlarged but fairly literal תיבין וכפלנין יתדהון כמא דפלנין אבריא לנודודא וחלקיא לנו קדרא. For *excoriaverunt* of common text and Comm., Cod. Amiat. has *expoliaverunt*, a reading which must be the result of correction.

V. 4. No alteration.

The Targ. modifies the anthropomorphic, "he will even hide his face," by its ויסלק שכנתיה מנהון. The LXX and Pesh. also have ἀποστρέψει for the same reason. Symm: has ἀλλὰ ἀποκρύψει. It is not quite clear whether Pesh. has been influenced by LXX in this, for although in several passages they have respectively the same words as they use here, yet at Job xiii. 24, xxxiv. 29, the Pesh. has the same word, where the Greek (Theod.) has κρύπτω.

It is impossible to believe that the ἐπ' αὐτούς at the end of the verse is original : מעלליהם was translated as adverb accus. by ἐν τοῖς ἐπιτηδεύμασιν. A corrector thought of עליהם, and put ἐπ' αὐτούς in the margin, whence it found its way into the text. Jerome's LXX had not the words. Holmes and Parsons mention "87, 97 (228 adscript. marg.) 310, Compl. Ald. Arm. M.S., Arm. Ed." as not containing them. The Pesh., as Sebök suggests, may have read באשר ; so also LXX, ἀνθ' ὧν ; the M. T. כאשר is better.

V. 5. No alteration.

Targ., *more suo*, supplies דשקרא after נבייא ; in this case unnecessarily, seeing that דמטען follows. It expresses fully what it conceives to be the interpretation of the obscure words הנשכים בשניהם וקראו שלום, "quod qui offert* eis convivium carnis, pacem ei vaticinantur." Like the Targ., the LXX supplies "upon him." The order of the words varies slightly, B having εἰρήνην ἐπ' αὐτόν, A, Ar., Jer., ἐπ' αὐτον εἰρήνην—the latter an alteration to give greater emphasies to the ἐπ' αὐτόν. The LXX understood

---

* *b* has מוביל, *a* and *r* have מוביל ; מוביל seems on the whole to go better with להון שרין, but there is little to choose between the readings.

the sense of the passage to be that the false prophets by proclaiming to their adherents a peace which they had not been commissioned to proclaim really brought war upon them; hence it omits אשר, renders יתן as passive by ἐδόθη, and the Ar., correctly giving its meaning, uses the 1st pers. sing. active :—" Et praedicant illi pacem quam non *indidi* in os eorum." Both here and at Jer. vi. 4, the Vulg. alone * brings out the force of the word קִדְּשׁ, " sanctificant"; it is a crusade. The Pesh. contents itself with repeating the verb it has used in the former clause, ܥܠܕܒܢܘܗܝ, one of the many borrowed from Greek.

V. 6. For חָשְׁכָה read חֲשֵׁכָה.

לילה in the first member seems to require a corresponding noun in the second: the LXX and Vulg. regarded חשכה as being such: no doubt they were correct, and חשכה is used in preference to חשך for the sake of assonance with לילה : the pointing should be חֲשֵׁכָה which is found in Gen. xv. 12, Isa. viii. 22 (Hitzig), whilst the form חָשְׁכָה does not occur. Although, however, the noun is correct, some of the arguments adduced in its favour are not to be relied on. Ryssel, for example, objects to the verb חָשְׁכָה that impersonals designating natural phenomena are in the masc. gender, an objection which will not hold good in face of תמטיר, Am. iv. 7 (*see* Ewald, § 295, *a*). Fuerst, also, refers to עזבה, Jer. xlix. 11, and עשקה, Isa. xxxviii. 14, as analogous formations to the noun חשכה. But the word in Jeremiah is the imper. of the verb (*see*

---

* Several MSS. of the LXX have ἡγίασαν, and Jerome's LXX also.

G

Ewald, § 228, b, Olshausen, § 234, a), and although Delitzsch looks on עשׁ as a noun, Cheyne agrees with Klostermann in treating it as imper. The Pesh. is the only Vers. which clearly took חשׁכה as a verb.

For the figures "night" and "darkness" the Targ. substitutes תבהתון and תתכנעון, for the latter of which the Polyg. has the inexact *erubescetis*. The next clause also is interpreted rather than translated by ותחפי עקא כקבלא ית נביי שקרא. The Polyg. omits *et* before *sol* both in Pesh. and Ar. Ar. follows A in preserving the same order, ὑμῖν ἔσται, in both clauses; B varies it.

V. 7. No alteration.

For the simple החזים LXX has οἱ ὁρῶντες τὰ ἐνύπνια: at Zech. x. 2 τὰ ἐνύπ. is used in connection with delusive predictions; it is inserted here to convey an unfavourable impression, just as in Targ. שקרא is added with the same object. The Pesh. and Vulg. supply the cognate accusative, "qui vident visiones." The Vulg. renders בשׁו and חפרו by the one word ".confundentur." The Targ. makes no distinction betwixt נביא and חזה: it leaves הקסם untranslated, and employs again the words used in v. 6, ויתכנעון מלאלפא, which the translator again misrenders, though now with a different word, "et pudefient, ita ut non doceant." ועטו על שׂפם כלם is explained by the Targ. ויתעטפון על שׂפם כאבלין כולהון. The Vulg. also understood it correctly, "et operient omnes vultus suos."*
The Pesh. confounds שׂפם with שׂפה, "et fascia obvol-

---

* More correctly in Cod. Amiat. and Comm., "vultus suos omnes."

ventur omnes super labiis suis." The LXX varies in its translation of this phrase in the various places where it occurs :—

Lev. xiii. 45, περὶ τὸ στόμα αὐτοῦ περιβαλέσθω :
Ezek. xxiv. 17, παρακληθῇς ἐν χείλεσιν αὐτῶν :
Ezek. xxiv. 22, ἀπὸ στόματος αὐτῶν παρακληθήσεσθε :
Micah iii. 7, καταλαλήσουσι κατ' αὐτῶν. *

The comparison of these passages shows that the translators of the prophets did not understand the general sense of the phrase, and that none of them distinguished שפם from שפה, unlike in this to the translator of 2 Sam. xix. 24, who renders ע׳ ש׳ by ἐποίησε τὸν μύστακα. And the same comparison, bringing out the diverse ways in which עטה was treated, frees us from the necessity of thinking with Schnurrer and others that in our passage καταλαλήσουσι κ.τ.λ. is a rendering of נטפו על נפשם or הטיפו: it is neither more nor less than an exposition of what they deemed the meaning, put into a shape which would harmonize well with the rest of the verse.

כי אין מענה אלהים. Targ. read as M. T., and expanded the phrase slightly: "quandoquidem non sit in eis spiritus propheticus a facie Domini:" the Vulg. translates M. T. literally: LXX, διότι οὐκ ἔσται ὁ ἐπακούων (Ἀ ἐπακούσων) αὐτῶν, vocalized differently מֲעֲנֶה אֲלֵיהֶם: and the Pesh. has a construction which came from a mixture of the M. T. and LXX, "quia non respondebit illis Deus." Against the LXX it is to be observed that the Hiph. does not appear to be used in the sense "to answer,"

---

* Symm., καὶ περιβαλοῦνται ἐπὶ τῶν χειλέων αὐτῶν πάντες.

whereas the noun מענה is common: that the construction of ענה with אל is not common, it being used in this same book of Micah with בְּ, vi. 3, and את, vi. 5, and in other places most frequently with the accusative: and that in the verse before us מַעֲנֵה אֱלֹהִים is very suitable.

V. 8. Not improbably ומשפט וגבורה is an early gloss. The Targ., Pesh. and Vulg. are renderings of the M. T. ואולם. The LXX ἐὰν μή is probably from אוּלַי*, which at Num. xxii. 33 they represent by εἰ μή: ἐὰν μή in our passage, according to Jerome's correct punctuation, introduces the continuation of the thought expressed in the foregoing verse, "non est qui exaudiat eos nisi ego implevero &c.," but the meaning thus gained is not nearly so good as that supplied by the M. T., which brings out the antithesis between the false prophets and the true one. Field points out that Symm. treated the first word of the verse as derived from אלם, *ligavit*: "ἐκωλύθη (s. συνεσχέθη) ἐγώ εἰμι κ.τ.λ." The LXX ἐμπλήσω supposes מלאתי to be Pi., probably because no preposition precedes כח. But the Kal, meaning "to be full of," is more often without than with the preposition.

There are some grounds for suspecting the genuineness of ומשפט וגבורה: the fact that the Ar. has no translation

---

* In Chwolson's paper on *The Quiescents*, translated in Hebraica, 1890, p. 94, attention is called to the fact that the form of the Arabic Accusative in *a*, as well as that in *am*, has survived in many Heb. adverbs. Have we a similar phenomenon here, a word in *a*, afterwards differentiated into two forms, יְ— and םְ—, with diverse meanings, and the distinction not recognised by the LXX?

of καὶ κρίματος καὶ δυναστείας seems to point to a recension of the Greek text from which these words were absent; Chrysostom x. 16 (Montfaucon's Edition), is cited in Holmes and Parsons as omitting καὶ κρίματος, and 23 as omitting the καὶ before δυναστείας : *r* of the Targ. has not the words corresponding to ומ׳ וג׳ : in the Heb. text ומ׳ וג׳ stand very awkwardly in their present position, and may well have been a gloss which at an early date crept into the text; they add little to the sense, and detract considerably from the vigour of the passage. The Targ., Pesh. and Vulg. have rendered את־רוח by the genitive or its equivalent: LXX ἐν πνεύματι is better: the Targ. enlarges slightly: "virtute spiritus prophetiae a facie Domini." The LXX and Targ. treat the collectives חטאתו and פשעי as plurals. Is the Ar. here again affected by the Pesh. in using a sing. for ἀσεβείας ?

V. 9. No alteration.

On καταλοίποι see v. 1. An example of the effort after variety of expression is furnished by ἡγούμενοι for ראשי here, compared with the ἀρχαί of v. 1. Cod. Amiat. and Comm. have *haec*, which is more likely to be the original form than the Sixtine *hoc*. Both for the partic. מתעבים and for the third pers. plu. יעקשו the LXX, Targ. and Pesh. use participles, on purpose, as it seems, to avoid a transition from 2nd pers. to 3rd and a loss of concinnity with v. 10. But the Vulg., and the Polyg. translators of Targ. and Pesh. have used 2nd pers. plu. for both words. And so strongly has the Polyg. translator of the Ar. been affected by the work done by his collaborators, that he has in both cases rendered the 3rd pers. plu. of the Ar. by 2nd pers. plu.

V. 10. For בָּנֶה read בָּנִים.

This is not one of the frequently occurring instances where the Verss. have a plu. whilst we may be sure that they are translating a collective sing. Such a transition as בנה involves would be too sudden even for the book of Micah. All the Verss. are against it. And if בנה was written *defective* the mistake would easily be made. A, by a scribe's blunder, omits Σιών, the eye being misled by the similarity of σευ. LXX and Targ., as is their custom with such words, have the plu. for עולה. All the Verss., except Pesh., have in one or other way reproduced the plu. form דמים, the Targ. very neatly by דם אשיר: this Vers. also, perhaps because it shrank from any reflection on Zion as a city, transfers the blood-stains to the houses of the individual sinners :—" Condentes domos suas in Sion cum sanguine effuso."

V. 11. No alteration.

LXX μετὰ δώρων, and Vulg. "in muneribus," for בשחד: none of the other Verss., not even the Ar., has plu. The Vulg. has been influenced by LXX, which is rendering *ad sensum*, just as at Ex. xxiii. 8, השחד is rendered τὰ δῶρα. 'Απεκρίνοντο is almost certainly the rendering of יורו, although it is not the word usually chosen for this purpose, ἀναγγείλωσιν, for example being found in the precisely parallel Deut. xxiv. 8. But the decisions of the priests were in response to questions addressed to them, so that "to answer" is a natural description of their procedure. Aq. and Symm. have ἐφωτίζον. ישענו is rendered by the same word ἐπανεπαύοντο, 2 Kings v. 18, vii. 2: Pesh. substitutes the explanatory ܥܕܟܠܗܘܢ: r of Targ. also has רחצין, for which a and b have the synonym with our Heb. word מסתמכין, a later attempt to come nearer the Heb. For the negative question הלוא וגו' the Pesh., as elsewhere, has the equivalent affirmative declaration. It can only be through inexactness that LXX has ἐν ἡμῖν for בקרבנו: this weightier form is wanted at the end of the clause, and the other Verss. recognise it. The Lond. Polyg. has the support of b and r in reading תיתי against a which has תעול: the latter may have arisen by mistake from תיתי עלנא. We must also follow these authorities in reading ונביהא, not ונביי שקרא; the parallels רישהא and כהנהא require it, and the change was made in order to obtain the familiar phrase. The Targ. on this verse softens the contemptuous יקסמו into מלפין, uses the general ממון for the specific מחיר, has its usual circumlocutions, מימרא דיי and שכנתא דיי for יהוה, and puts אמרין for the sake of clearness between the question asked and the assertion which flows out of the implied answer.

V. 12. No alteration.

The Ar. does not often so entirely forsake the LXX as to substitute a literal for a figurative expression as in this verse, where it has here put خرب for ἀροτριαθήσεται. The Targ. and Pesh. have no particle of comparison before שדה. The LXX and Vulg. supply ὡς and *quasi*. On ὀπωροφυλάκιον see i. 6: Hitzig and Steiner endeavour to account for the plu. in עיין, by the proximity of ת and ציון, the latter critic suggesting that this form of the word may be due to a transcriber; it is, however, impossible to decide conclusively either as to the original form or as to the cause of the difference betwixt this passage and Jer. xxvi. 18, where we have עיים. B has ὡς before ὀπωρ. and εἰς before ἄλσος. A reverses the order; the former, with which Jer. agrees, is probably correct, and would exactly correspond to the Heb. The Targ. and Vulg. interpret טור בית מקדשא by הר הבית and "mons templi," in much the same way as in the first clause the Targ. enlarges בגלליכם into בדיל חוביכון. The final words במות יער are very variously dealt with. The Vulg. has "excelsa sylvarum," a literal translation, save that the plu. sylv. is used for the sing. in order the better to bring out the sense. The Pesh. translates as though it read בית: this may have arisen from a mistaken repetition of the word which has just preceded, but it is more probably a correction due to the fact that the translator did not understand במ' יער and made it accord with בית יער, Isa. xxii. 8, where the words stand at the end of the verse as here, and are rendered by the same words in the Pesh., and as diversely in the other Verss. as במ' י' are here. The LXX and Targ. hang together, ἄλσος δρυμοῦ, חישת חורשא: these are renderings of the M. T., and it is just possible that the choice of the word ἄλσος is due to the presence of במות, ἄλσος being the ordinary word for אשרה, and these being set up on the "high places." The recurrence of this phrase at Jer. xxvi. 18, a quotation of our passage, is a sufficient testimony in its favour, and the fact that the Pesh. there is the same as here shows that its בית was not accidental. Except for a slight variation in the Ar. all the Verss. there repeat their renderings of Micah iii. 12.

CHAPTER IV.

V. 1. No alteration.

Here and Isa. ii. 2 the LXX departs somewhat from the Heb., but the variations do not discredit the M. T. It will be instructive to put together the Heb. and the Greek of the two passages:—

Isa. ii. 2.	Micah iv. 1.
והיה באחרית הימים נכון	והיה באחרית הימים יהיה
יהיה הר בית יהוה	הר בית יהוה נכון
בראש ההרים	בראש ההרים

Thus far they differ only in the position of נכון. But it is otherwise with the LXX:—

Isa. ii. 2.	Micah iv. 1.
ὅτι ἔσται ἐν ταῖς ἐσχάταις ἡμέραις ἐμφανὲς τὸ ὄρος κυρίου, καὶ ὁ οἶκος τοῦ θεοῦ ἐπ' ἄκρου τῶν ὀρέων.	καὶ ἔσται ἐπ' ἐσχάτων τῶν ἡμερῶν ἐμφανὲς τὸ ὄρος κυρίου, ἕτοιμον ἐπὶ τὰς κορυφὰς τῶν ὀρέων.

Clearly the translation in Micah has been much affected by that in Isaiah: the position of ἐμφανὲς shows this; so also does the omission of οἶκος from the first clause. After the word κυρίου they took different paths: the Isaiah passage, influenced by the structure of the next verse, brings in the בית which it had dropped before; the Micah one, because in its Heb. text נכון immediately follows יהוה,

translates it afresh by ἕτοιμον. At Isa. ii. 2, A and Ar. have ἄκρων, a correction to agree with ὀρέων. It can only be by a transcriber's error that the Ar. at Isa. ii. 2 has طاهرا *purus*, and here ظاهرا, *manifestus* *; the diacritical point should be restored in the former place. The Ar. in Micah has missed the intention of the LXX, and instead of keeping ἐμφ. and ἔτ. separated from each other has brought them together, " manifestus dispositus."

The next clause runs :—

<table>
<tr><td align="center">Isa. ii. 2.</td><td align="center">Micah iv. 1.</td></tr>
<tr><td align="center">ונשא הוא מגבעות ונהרו אליו
כל־הגוים</td><td align="center">ונשא הוא מגבעות ונהרו
עליו עמים</td></tr>
<tr><td>καὶ ὑψωθήσεται ὑπεράνω τῶν βουνῶν, καὶ ἥξουσιν ἐπ' αὐτὸ πάντα τὰ ἔθνη.</td><td>καὶ μετεωρισθήσεται ὑπεράνω τῶν βουνῶν, καὶ σπεύσουσι πρὸς αὐτὸ λαοί.</td></tr>
</table>

Even in these clauses, where the very words used prove that two different hands have been at work, the comparison of another Vers., the Pesh., shows how the Isaiah passage affected the treatment of Micah by the translators, for the Pesh. here, as well as there, is ܟܠܗܘܢ. No special feature is presented by the Targ. : for בית יהוה it employs the fuller בית מקדשא די״, and it interprets " peoples shall flow unto it," by " vultus vertent ut serviant super eo regna."

Justin Martyr's citation of this passage, as quoted by Field from Nobil., differs from the current text as well of Micah as of Isaiah : "ἕτοιμον ἐπ' ἄκρου τῶν ὀρέων, ἐπηρ-

---

* The Paris Polyg. prints as the Lond. in both places.

μένον αὐτὸ ὑπὲρ τοὺς βουνοὺς καὶ ποταμὸν θήσονται [fort., ποταμωθήσονται (וְנָהֲרוּ) . . .] ἐπ' αὐτῷ λαόι."

V. 2. No alteration.

A and Ar. repeat the πρὸς αὐτὸ of the foregoing clause, copying it, in all probability, by mistake. *Properabunt*, of the Vulg., intrinsically too strong a word, was chosen because it did not need the expression of a *terminus ad quem*. The omission of ו in the translations of ונעלה is idiomatic*, and does not imply that ו was absent from the text: לכו was looked on as a kind of exclamation: the Targ. retains the ו. This latter Vers. repeats the words of v. 1, בית מק' דיי מתקן. In the second half of the verse the parallel passages are again dissimilar:—

ויֹרנו מדרכיו καὶ ἀναγγελεῖ ἡμῖν τὴν ὁδὸν αὐτοῦ.—Isa. ii. 3.
ויורנו מדרכיו καὶ δείξουσιν κ.τ.λ.—Micah iv. 2.

As the Heb. now stands the difference betwixt ירנו and

---

* Prof. H. P. Smith (Hebraica, 1886, p. 76), criticising Ryssel asks, "But is it not more simple to suppose that a ו has been omitted or inserted in one of the two Hebrew texts, especially in immediate proximity to another ו as here?" He thinks it "more probable that one of these chances has influenced the text, than that the translators made more or less intentional changes in what they were trying to render." But this is too strong a statement of the case against those who differ from him. A rendering of לכו ונ' by δεῦτε ἀναβῶμεν ought scarcely to be characterized as an "intentional change:" it is the translators way of giving the sense. And some reference should be made to the parallel passage before a decision is come to. There we find the M. T. and the Targ. the same as here, and very probably the LXX also. For although B has δεῦτε καὶ ἀναβ., A omits the καὶ, and in this agrees with Pesh., Jer. and Ar., so that we may fairly conclude that the conjunc. was introduced later from the Heb.

יורנו is simply that one is written *plene* and the other *defective*, but the LXX plu. inclines one to think that their reading must have been ירונו. In any case the sing. must be retained, not only because of its presence in the parallel passage, but also because in both places the Verss. agree in so reading. In both passages the מ of מדרכיו is left unnoticed in the LXX, and the word treated as sing. The omission of the preposition is not surprising: at 1 Sam. xii. 23 והוריתי אתכם בדרך is rendered καὶ δείξω ὑμῖν τὴν ὁδὸν, and at Prov. iv. 11 בדרך חכמה הרתיך ὁδοὺς γὰρ σοφίας διδάσκω σε. Both the preposition and, consequently, the plu. are vindicated by the Verss. here and in Isa.: all have the plu., and all have the preposition, except the Vulg., which itself keeps it here, *de viis*, but at Isa. ii. 3 has *vias*. There is nothing noteworthy in the Targ.: its paraphrases are in its ordinary manner:—
מאורחן דתקנן קדמוהי for בית שכינת אלהיה for ב׳ אל׳; באולפן אירתיה for מדרכיו; בארחתיו for אולפן פתומא for דבר.

As the result of his comparison of this verse with Isa. ii. 3 Sebök suggests that ܠܗ݁ there should be altered into the ܠܗܿܒܐ which we have here. I find that Eg. has ܠܗ݁ but that Rich, Add., and Add. 14,432 (described in the Museum Catalogue as of the sixth cent.) agree in reading ܠܗܿܒܐ.

V. 3. No alteration.
Here again Micah and Isaiah diverge:
ושפט בין הגוים והוכיח לעמים רבים—Isa. ii. 4.
ושפט בין עמים רבים והוכיח לגוים עצמים עד רחוק.—
Micah iv. 3.

For ἕως εἰς μακράν of B, ἕως γῆν μακράν is found in A and "ἕως εἰς γῆν μακράν 26, 36, 40, 42, 49, 106, 153, 198, 233, Alex. Slav."* These, no doubt, were an attempted improvement on the translation of the harsh עד רח׳, for which the Targ. used עד עלמא: the Pesh. removed the roughness by bringing these words into grammatical connection with the words immediately preceding, "gentes potentes procul dissitas." It is an interesting illustration of the reciprocal action of the parallel passages that the Pesh. introduces this עד רח׳ into the corresponding verse in Isaiah, and on the other hand omits here the adjective רבים because it is not found there. In one point the Pesh. stands alone: it makes the *word* of v. 2 subject to שפט and הוכיח and in this respect differs from its treatment of Isaiah ii. 4.

A and B at Isa. ii. 4 have ζιβύνας: A here has ζιβύνας, but B has δόρατα; the ζιβ. of A has originated in the wish to harmonize with the other passage: the Ar. word here is not the same as in Isaiah, though synonymous, as indeed are δόρατα and ζιβύνας. The only point which raises a textual question in this second half of the verse is the יִשָּׂא in Isaiah compared with our יִשְׂאוּ. Some weight must be ascribed to the fact that all † the Verss. have the sing. here, for although, as we have seen, the translations of the one prophet are much affected by those of the other, yet this influence is not all-pervasive, and the

---

* Holmes and Parsons.

† Even the Targ., the common text of which, יטלון, is almost certainly a correction, occasioned by reference to the Heb., of the יטל found in *r*.

sing. of this word s perhaps the solitary instance in which all alike are in opposition to the M. T. On the other side it must be allowed that even the ישא of Isaiah may be plu., and that in both passages either number is grammatically admissible: the LXX have no scruple in rendering ישבו, v. 4, by the sing. ἀναπαύσεται because איש follows. If ישא in Isaiah is sing. the variation implied in our plu. will be quite in accord with the other results obtained by a comparison of the two versions of this prophecy preserved by Isaiah and Micah respectively; in this verse עד רחוק and עצמים are peculiar to Micah, he has ואל as compared with אל and חרבתיהם against חרבותם— all in the direction of greater fulness and explicitness. We must, therefore, although with some doubt, accept the M. T. The Ar. supports the simpler form of the LXX found in B, οὐκέτι μὴ . . . . οὐκέτι μὴ and not A's οὐκέτι οὐ μὴ . . . . οὐ μὴ μαθ. ἔτι.

In this verse, as compared with the corresponding one in Isaiah, עמים is always found in place of גוים, and *vice versâ*: the Pesh. does not distinguish between the words; it, however, and the Vulg. are more precise in the rendering of אתים than the ἄροτρα of LXX; they have respectively ܣܟܐ ܦܶܢ and *vomeres*, and probably the סכין of the Targ. should be taken as having the same force, equivalent to the fuller סיכת פדניא of 1 Sam. xiii. 21. *a* and *b* of Targ. read סיפין וזין: *r* has only זין as at Isa. ii. 4: סיפין וזין reads very awkwardly in this place: זין alone is probably original, and the סיפין was added later, at first as an alternative, and subsequently as an addition, by some one who wished to bring in the same word as had been used in the former clause. The Pesh., like the Targ., varies the word in the two clauses.

V. 4. No alteration.

LXX repeat ἕκαστος, and at end of verse have ταῦτα. Neither had its counterpart in the Heb., where the second איש can quite well be dispensed with, and דבר requires no object. The same is to be said of the ܒܠܗܘܢ after ܐܡܪ, and the plurals which the Pesh. has put for " vine " and " fig-tree." For these latter the Targ., " sub *fructu* vitis suae, subque fructu *ficulneae* suae " is singularly infelicitous. Its paraphrase of " the mouth of the Lord of Hosts hath spoken " by " by the Word of the Lord of Hosts it is determined thus," is no doubt an attempt to avoid a seeming anthropomorphism. *a* and *r* correctly read ויתבון, against יתובון of *b*, and at the end of the verse *r* has גזר not גור. For *vitem* Cod. Amiat. and the Comm. have *vineam*: the Comm. do not agree with Cod. Amiat. in omitting *suam* after *ficum*, or in using *quoniam* instead of *quia*. *Vinea* for *vitis* is not uncommon in Jerome and the Vulg.: see Isaiah xvi. 8, Hosea xiv. 8: it is found in Phaedrus in the same sense.

V. 5. No alteration.

No one can hesitate to prefer the איש בשם אלהיו of M. T., Pesh. and Vulg. to the ἕκαστος τὴν ὁδὸν αὐτοῦ of LXX.* The parallelism demands it: biblical writers were

---

* "'Άλλος· ἐν ὀνόματι θεοῦ (αὐτοῦ). Justin M., ἐν ὀνόματι θεῶν αὐτῶν."—*Field*.

not so afraid of appearing to admit the existence of other gods as the LXX were (see especially Deut. xxix. 26): the motive of the change is obvious, whereas no motive can be assigned that would have operated in the reverse direction: and the Targ., to which we naturally look for a similar evasion, has one which betrays the M. T. behind it, כל עממיא יהכון על די פלחו לטעותא.* In the next words בשמא of *a* and *r* is preferable to במימרא of *b*: no such reason as is given in v. 4 can be adduced to account for מימ׳ here: נתרחן for נלך is expository. Ar. does not agree with A in omitting κυρίου: so uncertain is the LXX in its employment or omission of divine names that it is impossible to assign reasons in each particular instance.

V. 6 and 7.   No alteration.

אספה הצלעה והנדחה אקבצה ואשר הרעתי ושמתי את הצלעה לשארית והנהלאה לגוי עצום. The Targ. and the Pesh. both have plurals and both are misled in their translation of צל׳ by the parallel נד׳. The Polyg. translator divides the words of the Targ. wrongly: he has "congregabo translatos et dispersos, colligam et illos quibus malefeci, &c.;" whereas, *colligam* is the verb that governs *dispersos*. Both for הנדחה and הנהלאה A has ἀπωσμένην, and B has ἔξω. and ἀπωσ. respectively: Jer. supports B in having two different words, but in this

---

* Notwithstanding the authority of *a* and *r*, which have יחובון, it is better to retain יהכון of *b*: יחובון as a rendering of ילכו is not easy to think of: it would be less likely to be corrupted into the weaker יהכון than reversely; indeed it is evident that יח׳ would appear much more vigorous, and therefore the preferable word.

instance A has preserved the original text: Zeph. iii. 19 ἀπωσ. is used by both A and B; here 'הנד and 'הנה are evidently regarded as corresponding to each other; and the ἔξωσ. of B is introduced partly for the sake of variety and partly as answering better to the Heb. καὶ οὓς ἀπωσάμην would at first sight lead us to think that some other verb such as הדחתי had been read for הרעתי, but the evidence of the other Verss.* is decidedly in favour of the M. T., and it would be impossible for the Massoretes to alter an inoffensive word like הדחתי into one carrying an association of evil with it, whereas it is easy to conceive of the LXX avoiding the unacceptable word. According to what is probably the true reading found in r the Targ. escapes attributing evil to God in another manner:—" and those to whom† evil has been done on account of the sins of my people." It is to be observed that the awkwardness of the clause ואשר הרעתי standing alone is got rid of in the Targ. by the addition, " on account &c." The Pesh. turns the corner of this same difficulty by omitting the conjunction and attaching אשר הר' directly to the foregoing: " dispersos recipiam, quibus malum intuleram." הנהלאה has given trouble to the translators. The LXX, as we have seen, proceed as though 'הנד were repeated: so also the Targ. This is to be explained by the facts that 'הנה is a peculiar word, ἀπ. λεγ., and that it stands in this verse in the position corresponding to הנד in v. 6. The

---

* Justin Martyr, quoted in full below, has καὶ ἦν ἐκάκωσα.

† איתבאש or, as Ryssel says, אתבאש, in place of אבאשית of *a* and *b*.

Pesh. retains in this verse its two words for הצל 'and הנד' in v. 6, but transposes them. The Vulg. has "quae laboraverat," from הנלאה, fem. Niph. partic. of לאה, just as at Isa. xv. 2 כי־נלאה is represented by "quod laboravit." All these phenomena are best accounted for by the translators having been unfamiliar with the word before them, and this is certainly one of the cases where we are not entitled to abandon the more difficult for the easier. Steiner's argument in favour of the Vulg. that it obtains a better contrast to גוי עצום, thought not destitute of force, is not strong enough to justify an alteration. For שמתי . . . . לשארית the Pesh. اܐܒܡ ܣܝܡ is a peculiar rendering, needing such an adjec. as the Polyg. translator has supplied; "Finem *faustum* faciam." The Pesh. is also peculiar in adding "and in Jerusalem," which came, no doubt, from the two, Jerus. and Mount Zion, being so often named together, as in iii. 12 and iv. 2. The Targ. avoids the idea that God's reign is a something that lies in the future; it is the manifestation thereof that has not yet been accomplished :—"Atque revelabitur regnum Dei super eos &c." By a scribe's error, Cod. Amiat. has *in montem* for *in monte*. B has ἕως εἰς τὸν αἰῶνα; A and Jer., probably a correction according to Heb., καὶ ἕως κ.τ.λ.

Justin's quotation of v. 6, given by Field, differs considerably from our current text: "συνάξω τὴν ἐκτεθλιμμένην, καὶ τὴν ἐξωσμένην ἀθροίσω, καὶ ἣν ἐκάκωσα :" this is nearer the Heb. and supplies evidence of the existence of a recension of the LXX unlike in many respects to the one preserved in our chief MSS.

V. 8. Omit תָאתֶה.

In this, as in other passages, the Verss. have confused עֹפֶל and אֹפֶל together: even Aq. has σκοτώδης and Symm. ἀπόκρυφος. At 2 Kings v. 24, where the M. T. has הָעֹפֶל the LXX has τὸ σκοτεινόν, the Targ. אֲתַר כָּסֵי, the Pesh. *latibulum montis*, the Vulg. *nebulosa*. And Geiger (p. 472) remarks on Num. xiv. 44: " leitet J. Th. 1 וַיַּעְפִּלוּ von אֹפֶל, Dunkel, ab, so auch Vulg.: contenebrati :" to which may be added that the Vulg. in that passage is all the more remarkable seeing that the LXX bears no trace of this interpretation but renders διαβιασάμενοι; and, further, that Jon. ben Uziel agrees with the Jer. Targ., the latter having וְיַעְפִּילוּ וְוֹרִיזוּ קֳדָם קְרִיצְתָא לְמֵיסוֹק and Jon. וְיַעְפִּילוּ וְאִזְדָּרְזוּ וגו'. There can be no doubt as to the correctness of the M. T. in our passage. The parallelism with מִגְדַּל is in its favour: if a second determinative, in addition to עֵדֶר, had been required it would have had the article (Ges. § 111, 2) הָאֹפֶל: the sense also is against אֹפֶל, for the prediction is a joyful one in which a sad epithet would be out of place : certainly the sense obtained by the LXX is an unsatisfactory one, making the "tower of the flock" one and the same with "the daughter of Zion," identifying thus the place and the people :—" Et haec turris filia est Sion: sive ut Symmachus vertit in Graecum : *Ipsa est filia Sion*," Jer. The Pesh. read רִעְה * for עֵדֶר, one of the instances in which the Targ. affected it indirectly but

---

* Ryssel is fully justified in vocalizing ܪܰܥܝܳܐ, not ܪܰܥܝܳܐ: the idea of the tower being pastured on is absurd.

none the less powerfully. The Targ. brings out the well-known Jewish belief that the revelation of the Messiah awaits the purging of Israel from its sins :—" And Thou, O Messiah of Israel, who art hidden because of the sins of the congregation of Zion:" the טמיר comes from אפל, and the משיחא from מגדל owing to the idea of protection and safety which is implied in the latter.

Ἐκ Βαβυλῶνος is obviously out of place :—" *Quod autem in quibusdam libris legitur: Et ingredietur principatus primus regnum filiae Sion, de Babylone.* Sciamus additum esse: quia nec in Hebraeo, nec apud alios habetur Interpretes." Jer. It was a marginal gloss partly suggested by ἥξεις ἕως Βαβυλῶνος below and partly by a reminiscence of Gen. x. 10.* Ryssel is no doubt correct in holding that תאתה is another marginal gloss which has crept into the text and brought with it the ו before באה: if repetition had been wanted for emphasis the stress would have been laid, not on the verb, as it now is, but on the noun; the important point is, "What is it that is coming?" The LXX ἐπὶ σὲ ἥξει, καὶ εἰσελεύσεται ἡ ἀρχὴ κ.τ.λ. shows that the תאתה found its present position at an early date, but is so awkward, leaving the subject unmentioned with the first verb,† and when it brings in the subject having a verb with no essential difference of meaning, that it cannot be regarded as a strong confirmation of the M. T. For עדיך the Pesh. read עתך,

---

* Note the similarity of language: here, ἡ ἀρχὴ ἡ πρώτη βασιλεία ἐκ Βαβ. : there, ἀρχὴ τῆς Βασ. αὐτοῦ Βαβυλών.

† The Targ. would not leave the verb thus: it therefore interpolated the subject, מלכותא.

perhaps, as Sebök thinks, from the ד and the י running together: Ryssel thinks we need not believe that they read otherwise than our M. T.: "indem man es wahrscheinlich für nächstverwandt mit עַד *Ewigkeit* oder gar mit עֵת *Zeit* hielt," and he supports this by the not very weighty consideration that the Targ. on Ps. ciii. 5 turns עֲדִי by יוֹמֵי סָבוּתִיבִי. But the Pesh. there does not follow the Targ. and a blunder of the latter at that place should not have much effect on our judgment of the Pesh. here. It is better to take ܩܪܒ intransitively as the Polyg. has done (appropinquavit), than to think of the Pesh. as reading the Hiph. here.* The ܫܘܠܛܢܐ of this Vers. seems to have been occasioned by the שָׁלְטוֹנָא of the ordinary text of the Targ., and this would make one slow to adopt the שׁוּלְטָנָא of *r*: besides which the latter is more like a correction according to Heb. The דישׂראל of *r* is also to be rejected; it is a mistake for דירושלם.

V. 9. No alteration.

עתה למה תריעי רע. LXX καὶ νῦν ἵνα τί ἔγνως κακά; they alone read ד for ר, ועתה למה תדעי רע. The Ar. mistook κακά here as meaning moral evils. The Targ. took the verb as equivalent to תרעה, and *may* have treated the רע as infin. †כען למה מתחברא לעממיא. At Prov. xxii. 11 they render חן ספתיו רעהו מלך by ובחסדא דשפוותיה יתחבר למלכא. The Pesh. read רָע תָּרֵעִי, and

---

* See Ryssel.

† So *r*: *a* and *b* have וכען, but this may be owing to the LXX καὶ.

the Vulg. probably תַּרְעִי רַע. The M. T. is better than any of these. Zion's cry is quite in place, seeing that at the end of this verse she is compared to a travailing woman. It is not certain that the LXX read ועתה; they might prefer to introduce the question with καὶ, and in any case they stand alone, with the doubtful exception of the Targ. The μὴ βασιλεὺς οὐκ ἦν σοι does not imply any other reading than בך: at Jer. viii. 19 we have the precisely similar אם־מלכה אין בה, and this passage confirms the M. T. of the preceding words because although it does not use הָרִיעַ it distinctly mentions the cry of the people :—" Behold, the voice of the cry of the daughter of my people .... Is not her king in her?" The Vulg. has been influenced by the LXX: "numquid rex non est tibi &c?" יועץ is usually rendered σύμβουλος, and βουλή, as at Isa. xix. 11, is the rendering of עצה. But such a passage as Prov. xi. 14, ברב יועץ, ἐν πολλῇ βουλῇ, to say nothing of the more difficult פלא יועץ אל, Μεγάλης βουλῆς ἄγγελος, Isa. ix. 5, shows that the LXX need not have read any differently from the M. T. in our passage. They probably chose the abstract βουλή with the idea that a new idea, not parallel to the former one, is being brought in. Targ. and Pesh. have plurals, the former in a very emphatic manner, מלכי מילכיך. The LXX treats this second question as extending to the end of the verse, and the Ar. goes further still and regards the whole as equivalent to an affirmation*:—" Consilium tuum periit, quod occuparint se dolores similes doloribus parturientis." For the simple חול the Targ. has עקא וזיע.

---

* One of the errors incident to a translation of a translation.

V. 10.   No alteration.

נוח is not often used, and this may account for the variety of translations. For the words חולי וגחי the Targ. has מרע וזועי, where the verb זוע corresponds to the noun זיע in v. 9, and is used because the Targumist thought a word allied in meaning to חול was wanted. This is the explanation also of the Vulg. "satage." Cod. B has ὤδινε καὶ ἀνδρίζου καὶ ἔγγιζε; A, 87*, 91, alii, and Jer. ὤδινε καὶ ἀνδρίζου; Ar. omits ὤδινε and for the rest agrees with B. Ryssel thinks ὤδ. καὶ ἀνδ. a double translation of חולי, the ἀνδ. being from a denominative assumed to belong to חַיִל, or else from חִיל, "to be strong"; ἔγγιζε from גשי or געי (mistakenly read in place of גחי) would afterwards be dropped out of the text owing to its being noticed that two imperatives, corresponding to the two Hebrew imperatives, were already there. This explanation is not unreasonable if it mean that the καὶ ἀνδ. was a marginal reading intended as an alternative to ὤδινε, and afterwards finding its way into the text. But the two renderings are so unlike in meaning that they certainly cannot have been originally intended to stand together. Is it possible that ἀνδρίζομαι was used in this provincial dialect in the sense, not very far removed from its common one, of "to bring forth a man"? If it were, ὤδινε κ. ἀνδ. would be the rendering of חולי וגחי, and καὶ ἔγγ. a marginal reading, a translation of געי.

שם תנצלי שם יגלך. Both times LXX has ἐκεῖθεν, in accordance with the interpretation which it deems correct: before the second one it has καὶ; Pesh. has this before each; so have *a* and *b* of Targ., but *r*, like M. T., neither time: the middle ῥύσεται is for the sake of conformity to λυτρώσεται. LXX adds ὁ θεός σου.

V. 11. No alteration.

Pesh. omits the ו before עתה in conformity with v. 9: none of the rest do so. ἐπισυνήχθη ... οἱ λέγοντες of A, Ar. and Jer. (the latter two, at all events so far as the οἱ goes) looks like a correction of B's text ἐπισυνήχθησαν .... λέγοντες; the first correction unnecessary, because the plu. could well be used by a *constructio ad sensum*, the second being an improvement, because the ה of M. T. and remaining Verss. makes a real difference in the meaning.

תחנף ותחז בציון עינינו. Pesh. differs from M. T. only in putting Zion into immediate connection with the first verb, so as to show at once what the subject of the sentence is, and in having the sing. "eye" to agree with the verb. The Targ. turns the phrase, so as to get a powerful testimony to Zion's purity:* "Quando impie aget, et videbit ruinam Sion oculus noster?" It also, as well as the Vulg., has the sing. "eye." The Vulg. has: "Lapidetur, et aspiciat in Sion oculus noster." It is impossible to suggest another verb as likely to have been before the translator. Jerome's note, "Gentes multae, quae quasi de adultera loquuntur, et dicunt: *Lapidetur* &c.," goes a considerable distance towards proving that *Lapidetur* is a free rendering of תחנף, the stoning being the consequence of the pollution. It is possible, Ryssel thinks it likely, that a similar explanation must be given of the LXX

---

* *a* omits אימתי, possibly because it was observed that there is no query in the Heb.

Ἐπιχαρουμεθα, which he regards as a free translation, adopted because of the meaning of the next clause: I am not satisfied with this but cannot suggest a word which the LXX may have read instead of תחנף. Field represents Symm. as using κατακριθήσεται or καταδικασθήσεται. In καὶ ἐπόψονται ἐπὶ Σιὼν οἱ ὀφθαλμοὶ ἡμῶν, they put the verb in the plu. Neither this nor the change to "eye," sing., is needful in Heb. (Ewald, § 317, 1; Ges. § 146, 3.).

V. 12. No alteration.

LXX and Pesh. translate מחשבות by the sing. In other passages they render, now by the plu. now by the sing., the latter, for example, Jer. xi. 19, xxix. 11. Targ. has רויא, a rendering the genesis of which is well brought out in Dr. Hatch's note on μυστήριον*:—" It is frequently used in the Apocryphal books .... in a majority of passages of secrets of state, or the plans which a king kept in his own mind. This was a strictly Oriental conception. A king's 'counsel' was his 'secret,' which was known only to himself and his trusted friends. It was natural to extend the conception to the secret plans of God." It is not without interest to note this similarity in mode of thought between the Targumist and the Jews who wrote Greek.

Ryssel's remark, "Das Nennwort עמיר wird von Vulg. sonderbarer Weise durch Heu wiedergeben," loses some of its force when it is remembered that *foenum* is the ordinary rendering of עמיר: see Jer. ix. 22, Amos ii. 13, Zech. xii. 6. Aq. and Symm. have ἄχνη; Theod. καλάμη.

---

* Essays in Biblical Greek, p. 58.

V. 13. For וְהַחֲרַמְתִּי read וְהַחֲרַמְתְּ.

For the figurative דוּשִׁי the Targ. has the literal קְטֹלִי: it and the Vulg. abstain from adding the object which LXX and Pesh. give. LXX has τὰ κέρατα . . . σιδηρᾶ, thinking both horns needed mention, which is not the case in the O. T. The Pesh. has the plu. "horns," but for iron and brass retains the sing. nouns: "das Semitische von Stoffwörtern nicht gern Adjectiva bildet". Ewald. The Vulg. has *cornu*. The Targ paraphrases: "populum enim qui in te est, ponam fortem sicut ferrum." Here again the Pesh. affects Ar., occasioning the omission of the second אָשִׂים. The Targ. interprets this clause:— "Et reliquias eorum robustas sicut aes." Pesh. alone omits the ו of וְהֲדִקּוֹת: Targ. renders this word, like דוּשׁ, by וּתְקַטְלִין: B has κατατήξεις, and A and Jer. λεπτύνεις, the latter probably an improvement suggested by the Heb. The Ar. here has come from λεπτύνω, but it is remarkable as being the cognate word (داس) to the דוּשׁ at the beginning of the verse. There can be no doubt that the second pers., וְהַחֲרַמְתְּ, must be adopted. It is Jahweh who is strengthening his people; it is to him that the spoils are to be devoted; the assertion that He will devote them to himself would be out of place. Cod. Amiat. of Vulg. is the only place in the Verss. where the first pers., *interficiam* is used: and this can hardly be original: the ordinary text has *interficies*; so also the Comm., both in its text and, as far as can be judged, in its notes: when it is said that *interficiam* was probably altered to *interficies* because of the meaning, there seems just as much force in the reply that the reverse change may have been made in deference to the Heb. text, in the same manner as the ותגמרין of *b* and *r* has been changed in *a* to ואגמר. For there is no reason to doubt that the י was written, although the 2nd pers. was intended. Ewald says: "Die gelehrtere (etymologische), Schreibart תי (aus dem ursprünglichen *ti*) im Aramaischen treuer erhalten, findet sich in H. L., ferner Micah iv. 13 (wo die Massôra תי liest, und wohl anders erklärt) sodann vorzüglich bei Späteren." See also Chwolson, *Hebraica*, 1890, p. 108.

בצעם is variously, and, on the whole, not very appropriately rendered. We are not surprised that this should be the case in the LXX with its τὸ πλῆθος αὐτῶν, seeing that it has elsewhere such a variety of translations, χρήσιμον, ὑπερηφανία, δῶρον, πλεονεξία, ὠφέλεια. The Targ. has נכסהון, with which the Pesh. corresponds. The Vulg. plu. *rapinas* is probably to mark the concrete sense in which it is used, as well as because of the plu. suffix. The Targ. seems to shrink from the thought that destruction could be directly *for* Jahweh: it therefore runs "consumes autem coram Domino." The LXX τὴν ἰσχὺν αὐτῶν and Vulg. "fortitudinem eorum" miss the sense of חילם which Targ. and Pesh. have seized: the Targ. amplifies slightly:—"Et pretiosam eorum pecuniam coram dominatore universi mundi." In this paraphrase we see עלמא losing its strict original signification, and becoming a mere equivalent of ארץ: much the same kind of change as αἰών underwent.

V. 14. Probably שָׁמוּ should be read for שָׁם
Two considerations are decisive against the LXX de-

parture from the M. T. in the first clause of this verse; first, the unanimity of the other Verss., which differ indeed in their interpretation but agree in proceeding from the M. T., and, secondly, the position of the word בת which the LXX itself bears witness to, תתגדדי בת גדוד; it could not have stood thus unsupported midway between the verb and the noun cognate thereto. No doubt the rendering Νῦν ἐμφραχθήσεται θυγάτηρ ἐμφραγμῷ has arisen partly from the feeling that something intimately connected with a siege is being spoken of, as well as from the similarity of the letters in the two words גדד and גדר. The Kal of this latter is rendered φράσσω at Hosea ii. 8. A, followed by Ar., has ἐφραὶμ ἐνφραγμῷ, a copyist's reduplication. The Vulg., "Nunc vastaberis, filia latronis," is a rendering of the M. T.:—"Hoc juxta Hebraicum: cui interpretationi Aquila et Symmachus et Theodotio, et editio Quinta consentiunt;" the *f. latronis* being a literal rendering of בת גד׳ as at Hosea vi. 9 איש גדודים is *virorum latronum*, and the *vastaberis* reminding us of the *incido* which is used for התגדד, 1 Kings xviii. 28. The Targ. and Pesh. resemble each other in showing their sense of the looseness of structure which makes this verse a difficult one, but differ in their detailed treatment of it; the former, reading the M. T., ran two clauses into one :—
* "Nunc per turmas sociaberis, civitas, quam obsidione obsidebant illi." The Pesh., "Nunc prodibis cum turma, O filia turmarum potentium," attaches to this clause the מצור of the next, and by reduplication of the מ of this

---

* *a*, like the Ar., begins the verse with ו, in conformity with v. 11.

word makes the preceding one into גְדוּדִם. It is not absolutely necessary to suppose that Pesh. thought of מִבְצָר instead of מָצוֹר, because although 'מב is the word thus rendered, e.g. Jer. iv. 5. xxxiv. 7, yet 'מע is treated as almost equivalent to 'מב in such passages as Zech. ix. 3.

There is a closer connection between the Targ. and Pesh. in their treatment of מָצוֹר שָׂם עָלֵינוּ than the Polyg. "quam obsidione obsidebant illi" and "quia insurrexerunt in nos" exhibits: the relative pron. in the Syr. is, in this case, not well represented by *quia*; it refers to the *turmae potentes* just mentioned. The verb used in the Pesh. ܡܥܒܕ does not imply that anything different from שָׂם was read: the more forcible word had become necessary because מָצוֹר had been lost from this clause. Both these Verss. and the Vulg. read שָׂמוּ: the LXX has the sing. Jerome's words, above quoted, appear to claim for this as well as for the rest of the Vulg. rendering the authority of the Heb. and of the other Greek translators. On the whole the evidence preponderates in its favour. It may, of course, be urged that the change to the plu. would be an obvious one for a corrector to make, because יכו follows, but on the other hand the plu. seems to be required for this word as much as for that, the same subject being intended, and the LXX sing. can be accounted for by the well-warranted assumption that שָׂם only was written, leaving the vowel-letter ו to be supplied.

For שפט ישראל the LXX read 'שבטי יש or, taking the governing noun as a collective, 'שבט יש. They were misled by the שבט in the line above: a representative person, "the judge of Israel," could be smitten on the cheek; not so "the tribes of Israel:" the Verss. support the M. T., the Targ. having, indeed, the plu. דיני, according to its wont, and the Pesh. translating שפט not literally but by ܢܟܐ;. Aq., Symm. and Theod. have τὸν κριτήν. The sing. σιαγόνα is found in B, Jer., Ar.: the σιαγόνας of A is due to φυλὰς.

The Ar. rendering of συνοχὴν ἔταξεν ἐφ' ἡμᾶς (ὑμᾶς of A must be a transcriber's error) is another good example of the distance to which a translation of a translation may travel from the original: a slightly different turn is given to the meaning of τάσσω; consequently συνοχή is wrongly rendered and we get رتّب علينا لزوما, *praescript nobis decreta*.

CHAPTER V.

V. 1. For אֶפְרָתָה צָעִיר read אֶפְרַת הַצָּעִיר: omit לִהְיוֹת.

Seeing that אפרת is the proper form of the word and that אפרתה, even if it were retained, could only be explained as a corruption which has arisen from this townname having been used several times with the ה of motion towards, there is good reason for Hitzig's conjecture that the ה is the article belonging to the next word: an excellent connection is thus obtained: "And thou, Bethlehem Ephrath, the little one in &c.," or, "who art little in &c.".

No satisfactory explanation has been given of the LXX βηθλεὲμ οἶκος 'Εφραθά. The best suggestion would be that two readings of the Heb. text at one time were current and have here found a place side by side, were it not that Ephrath, not Beth-Ephrath, is the shape in which the word elsewhere appears. This objection applies also to the idea that Beth-Eph. is original and *lechem* a gloss which found its way into the text and led to the repetition (in translation) of the Beth. On the other hand it is next to incredible that the LXX should have arbitrarily inserted οἶκος. Perhaps the simplest way of treating the matter is to accept the M.T. as original, and to hold that in the Heb.

text which the LXX used a בית stood before 'אף, having been interpolated either accidentally or in the belief that the Eph. was parallel to the *lechem* and equally needed a Beth before it. There is nothing in the usage of other passages to render the appositional Bethlehem Eph. suspicious, and the remaining Verss. agree with the M. T. The Polyg. translator gives *oppidum* for ܟܦܪ: there is a various reading in the MSS of the Pesh., Rich and Add. having ܟܦܪ, Eg. ܟܦܪ.

For ὀλιγοστὸς εἶ τοῦ εἶναι κ.τ.λ. of A and B many MSS. have μὴ ὀλ. εἶ κ.τ.λ.; a question which expects a negative answer and thus corresponds to the quotation in St. Matt. ii. 6, οὐδαμῶς ἐλαχίστη εἶ: the Ar. and Jer. translate the same text as we find represented in St. Matt., except that they did not omit the τοῦ εἶναι and that they adhered to χιλιάσιν against ἡγεμόσιν. The concessive ὀλιγ. εἶ was replaced in the first instance by a question, and this in turn gave place to a negative declaration of precisely the same import as itself, but of exactly opposite meaning to the Heb. and the original Greek. Like St. Matt. the Vulg. omits להיות, and although the Targ. and Pesh. support it there can be little doubt that Cheyne is right in thinking that it came in by mistake from the line below: צעיר להיות, *too small to be*, "is not strictly in accordance with grammar," צ׳ מהיות being much more idiomatic.

The next clause in B and Jer. runs: ἐκ σοῦ μοι ἐξελεύσεται τοῦ εἶναι εἰς ἄρχοντα τοῦ Ἰσραήλ: A has ἐκ σοῦ μ. ἐξ. ἡγούμενος τ. ε. εἰς ἄρχ. ἐν τῷ Ισραηλ, a confluent reading, τοῦ εἶ. ἡγ. ἐν τῷ Ἰσ. having been put into the marg. of a codex which read like B and afterwards passing into the text. The Ar. is a mixed text, in parts resembling A and in parts B, seeming also to bear at least one trace of St. Matthew's influence, ܠܝ corresponding to the γὰρ. St. Matt. has ἐκ σοῦ γὰρ ἐξελεύσεται ἡγούμενος, ὅστις ποιμανεῖ τὸν λαόν μου τὸν Ἰσ. The influence which the N. T. had on the Verss. of the O. T., and the LXX on the MSS. of the N. T. might well be illustrated by this quotation: the γὰρ, for example, has nothing corresponding to it in either the Heb. or the principal codices of the LXX; it is, therefore, omitted here in א¹, although there can be no doubt of its genuineness, the sense ascribed to the passage as a whole requiring it, and its presence having affected the Ar. translator of Micah: again the לִי of Micah is quite naturally left out in St. Matt.; this has led to the same omission by the Pesh. at Micah v. 1, but on the other hand its presence in the LXX of that passage has led to the insertion of μοι in St. Matt. by "CK[Γ] arm Protev-2-mss Thdrt:"* not improbably, also, the ὅστις ποιμανεῖ τὸν λ. μ. κ.τ.λ. is a reminiscence of the καὶ ποιμ. τὸ ποίμνιον αὐτοῦ of Micah v. 3.

It is not easy to account for the departure of the Ar. from its model in the last clause: in place of ἀπ' ἀρχῆς it has *in Israele*: possibly the Ar. text is corrupt, and these words, which have been used just before, have got into their present position by mistake. The sing. ܡܠܟܐ was occasioned by the verb from which this comes having been used just before and the clause in which the noun

---

* Alford's Greek Test., i. 13.

occurs being taken as the exposition of the one in which the verb has been employed. The Targ. on the latter half of this verse is a highly characteristic one: "Ex te coram me prodibit Christus, ut sit dominium exercens in Israel, cujus nomen dictum est ab aeternitate a diebus seculi:" the goings forth from Bethlehem of the destined ruler is an eternal counsel of God; there is no need to refer* to such passages as Num. xxx. 13, where מוצא (but always, be it observed, in conjunction with שפתים) means "that which goeth out of the lips." *r* is to be followed in its readings in this verse: it, with *b*, has כזעיר against דזער of *a*; it alone has ודי against די of *a* and *b*.

V. 2. No alteration.

Only the LXX and the Vulg. agree with the Heb. יתנם in having the sing. verb and also with its לכן. The Targ. has יתמסרון: the Pesh. has indeed the third pers. sing., but to emphasize the idea that the giving up is only temporary has substituted עתה for לכן: even the Ar. has a variation, using the sec. pers. sing. fem. so as to make Bethlehem the subject: all alike were unwilling to ascribe desertion of the people to him who has just been designated the ruler of the people. "Tradentur tempore quo parturiens pariet," in the Polyg., is not a good translation of יתמסרון כען ילדתא למילד, which means "They shall be given up as in the time when the travailing woman is about to bring forth." B and Jer. punctuate τικτούσης, τέξηται: A and Ar., correctly, and in accordance with

---

* Ryssel's alternative explanation.

Targ., Pesh. and Vulg., as well as M. T., τικτούσης τέξεται: it is the conciseness of the Heb. which has led to misapprehension.

Τῶν ἀδελφῶν αὐτῶν: Jer. omits αὐτῶν, leaving it an open question whose brethren they were : Ar. has αὐτῶν: Targ. plu. pron.: Pesh. and Vulg. agree with M. T., as do also Aq., Symm. and Theod. There can be no doubt that these latter are correct. The change to the plu. has been made to prevent even apparent depreciation of those who are connected with the Messiah. And the Targ. could not understand a distinction being drawn between "his" or "their brethren" and "the children of Israel": hence its עליהון, and its making בני יש׳ an apposition to שאר אח׳.

V. 3. For וְיָשְׁבוּ read יָשְׁבוּ and attach it to the middle clause of the verse.

LXX καὶ στήσεται καὶ ὄψεται, καὶ ποιμανεῖ τὸ ποίμνιον αὐτοῦ ἐν ἰσχύϊ κύριος. τὸ π. αὐτοῦ has been supplied as the suitable object to ποιμανεῖ, after the analogy of Isa. xl. 11, and it is quite possible that the recollection of that passage, where κύριος is the subject to ποιμανεῖ, and μετὰ ἰσχύος also appears, has had something to do with the mistaken arrangement adopted here. For it certainly is mistaken: יהוה as subject at the very end of the clause would be in a position of inexplicable emphasis: moreover the parallelism of בעז יהוה with בגאון שם י׳ א׳ would be spoiled. As to the καὶ ὄψεται the obvious account of its origin is that it is the translation of an erroneous variant ראה which was first placed in the margin and afterwards in the text. There is very little to be said for Ryssel's opinion that ὄψ. is a second translation of רעה in accordance with the etymology of the Heb. word, ποιμ. being according to the *usus loquendi*.

In its treatment of the remainder of the verse the LXX has preserved one original reading which the M. T. had lost. It has ישבו in place of וישבו, and gives this verb to the second clause as a parallel to those in the first and third clauses respectively, καὶ ἐν τῇ δόξῃ ὀνόματος κυρίου θεοῦ αὐτῶν ὑπάρξουσι. Unquestionably Prof. Smith is right in maintaining that the conjunction is due to reduplication from אלהיו. וישבו is altogether too abrupt to stand alone: if it belonged to a separate clause it would need some such modification as לָבֶטַח. The Targ. felt this roughness and endeavoured to avoid it: "atque convertentur de medio captivitatis suae," where the word is vocalized יָשׁוּבוּ; the Pesh. pointed like the Targ., but had no supplement: the Vulg. did the same, but Jerome's note shows that he was not satisfied: "Et convertentur, sive ut melius interpretatus est Symmachus, *habitabunt*. JASUBU* enim verbum Hebraicum utrumque significat." So far, however, as the suffix pronoun is concerned it is more advisable to adhere to the M. T. אלהיו than to adopt the LXX אלהיהם: the former explains the origin of וישבו, and it is supported by the remaining Verss.: the latter is easily accounted for as originating in the desire

---

* The closing remark on Jasubu is inexact: it ignores the difference between יָשׁוּבוּ and יֵשְׁבוּ or, at all events, vocalizes the Sheva of the latter word in accordance with the final ו, and does not take account of the fact that what in this case is derived in the other is original.

for conformity with the plu. verbs in this and the next clause. And in the next clause the sing. יגדל of the M. T. and other Verss. is preferable to the plu. μεγαλυνθήσονται of the LXX: it does not yield a good sense to say that their dwelling in the glory of the name of his God depends on *their* being magnified to the ends of the earth, whereas the magnifying of their prince may well tell on their fortunes: the Targ. is in the right when it interprets the saying of Messiah's fame: "nam magnificabitur nomen ejus usque ad fines terrae." Symm. also has μεγαλυνθήσεται.

V. 4. For אשור כי־יבוא read כִּי יָבוֹא אַשּׁוּר.

וְהָיָה זֶה שָׁלוֹם. The Vulg., "et erit iste pax," makes the Messiah the subject of the clause: the Pesh. omit זה and appears to connect "et erit pax" with the foregoing: the Targ., like the Pesh., does not directly refer the prediction to the Messiah, ויהי מבכן שלמא יהי *לנא: B has the impossible καὶ ἔσται αὐτῇ εἰρήνη: Ar. and Jer. αὐτὴ ἡ εἰρήνη; and no doubt St. Paul was referring to this prophecy in his αὐτὸς γάρ ἐστιν ἡ εἰρήνη ἡμῶν, where he may have had in mind a traditional rendering αὐτὸς, nearer to the Heb. than the αὐτὴ of the LXX, and a traditional ἡμῶν corresponding to the לנא of the Targ.

אשור כי־יבוא בארצנו. اذ is almost certainly a transcriber's mistake for اذا: Sebök cites "Cer. und Syr-Hex" in favour of the correction, but the three MSS. which I have examined, Rich., Add. and Eg., agree with the text. Targ., Pesh., B and Jer. begin the clause with

---

* So r: a and b have not יהי.

אשור: the Vulg. in all probability agreed with them, for although the Sixtine has *cum venerit-Assyrius*, Cod. Amiat. and the Comm. begin with *Assyrius*: A and Ar. have ὅταν Ἀσσύριος, which is certainly an emendation: in spite of the practical unanimity of the Verss. it is impossible to believe that even a crisis as great as the Assyrian one could produce this remarkable arrangement of the words, and the fact that we have מאשור כי־יבוא just below, where the order is quite correct, shows the origin of our text; כי יבוא אש׳ was originally written; the alteration was due to a mistaken copying of or intentional conforming to the phrase below.

וכי ידרך בארמנותינו. With this all the Verss. coincide, except the LXX which read אדמה in place of ארמון and, as in the previous clause, ὑμῶν for ἡμῶν: so far as the latter point is concerned, it need only be said that the change is in harmony with the manner in which the LXX avoid the first pers. in the verb (on which see below) and that the Ar. here, feeling the impropriety of the 2nd pers., has used the 1st, following, no doubt, the Pesh. In favour of אדמה it has been urged, but not proved, that the idea to be expressed is the rout of the Assyrian as soon as he sets foot in the land and before he has gained a footing in the palaces. And it has been attempted to support this by comparing the next verse, and so forming the parallels גבולנו ‖ אדמתנו, ארצנו ‖ ארצנו: but if an argument be based on this it must be conceded that it is not very powerful seeing that the parallels are not exact. It would need much strong reasoning to induce us to set aside the rarer ארמון in favour of אדמה.

Ἐπεγερθήσονται for הקמנו is for the purpose of avoiding the idea that the deliverance originated with the people themselves: an alteration with this object is far more likely than one in the opposite sense. δήγματα ἀνθρώπων is an interesting example of a mistake originating in similarity of sound, נשיכי being read for נסיכי. Jerome's note shows that the other Greek Verss. were more careful: "Ubi nos posuimus *primates homines*: et in Hebraico scriptum est NESICHE ADAM, Symmachus interpretatus est *Christos hominum*; Theodotio et Quinta Editio *principes hominum*. Aquila *graves*, vel *constitutos homines*, id est, κατεσταμένους." And it is even more interesting to note that the Ar. has given the rendering عظماء, *primates*. The Targ. and the Pesh. have the same word, רברבי. The פרנסין of *r* in place of מלכין of *a* and *b* as translation of רעים looks like an emendation made by a later Targumist, to whom the setting up of seven *kings* seemed an unfortunate expression and an unsatisfactory translation.

V. 5. For בִּפְתִיחָה read בְּפִתָחֶיהָ.

The Verss. correctly take רעו to be 3rd pers. plu. perf. of רעה: there is, of course, a reference to רעע, but רעה is bitterly ironical. The Pesh. نوبحون is merely an error of transcription for نوبعون: there is nothing to recommend أزي. It is impossible to decide whether את־ארץ has been accidentally omitted by the LXX through its similarity to אשור or, on the contrary, inserted in the Heb. for the sake of parallelism with the next words: the other Verss. have it. בפתחיה has occasioned much perplexity and can hardly be uncorrupt. The Targ. has " in fortitudine turrium ejus," a rendering which fails altogether to throw light on the text: the utmost that can be said is that they may have had the M. T. before them, and have looked on the entrances to the land as meaning the strong fortresses by which it was defended. A similar remark applies to ܒܟܘܡܗ of Pesh., a despairing attempt to find something harmonizing with the verse as a whole. Jerome's note is: "In eo ubi ego et Aquila transtulimus, *in lanceis ejus*, ut subaudiatur terrae Nemrod; Symmachus vertit ἐντὸς πυλῶν αὐτῆς, id est, *intra portas ejus*; Theodotio, *in portis eorum*; Quinta Editio, ἐν παραξίφεσιν αὐτῶν, quod nos possumus dicere, *in sicis eorum*: In Hebraeo autem positum est BAPHETHEE." All these would seem to have read alike, for the plu. pron. of Theod. and Quinta in all probability does not imply a plu. in their Heb. text. And the LXX ἐν τῇ τάφρῳ αὐτῆς seems to differ from their reading only in having the sing. of the noun. The questions remain, "What was their reading, and was it the original one?" I think פתח explains the LXX quite as well as the פחת which has been suggested, and the latter neither gives a good sense in this connection nor is elsewhere translated τάφρος. But the true explanation of the whole is that furnished by the parallelism: a word corresponding to "sword" is wanted: Jerome and the other Greek Verss. felt this and only erred in thinking a suffix pron. was here: at Ps. lv. 22 * פתיחה is interpreted as a weapon by all the Verss.: the reading בפתיחה here explains the variation between LXX

---

* "פתיחה ist das ausgezogene gezückte Schwert:" Del. *in loc.*

and the other Greek Verss. as to the num. of the noun, and when once the change from פתיחה to פתחיה had been made it would be inevitable that the latter part of the word should be looked on as suffix pron. The Ar. departs from its model in inserting *"them"* after *"he shall deliver;"* in following the other Verss. rather than the LXX with respect to the pronoun, *our* not *your;* and in omitting Asshur, this latter probably being a mere error. It will be noted that the LXX *your*, in both places of this verse, is to harmonize with the *your* of v. 4. The Targ. and Pesh. hang together in their treatment of the latter half of the verse: they boldly altered the כי־יבוא because they could not see the propriety of the repeated mention of the Assyrian coming into the land:—"Ut non ingrediatur in terram nostram, nec calcet terminos nostros;" "ne veniat in patriam * nostram, neque gradiatur, &c." Baer and Delitzsch's notes on this verse show that נמרד should be written *defective* and בנבולינו *plene*.

V. 6. No alteration.

There is a great difference between the aspect of Israel towards other nations as portrayed in this and the next verse respectively, quite great enough to account for the omission here of the בנים, which is found there. M.T., Targ. and Vulg. are therefore probably correct, and the Pesh. departure from them is due to the influence of the LXX. In both verses the Pesh. has the sing., owing no doubt to the fact that it renders עמים by the same word

---

* On ڱل see v. 4.

and wants the plu. for it because it is accompanied by רבים. It is not likely that the LXX ἄρνες is founded on a reading כבישים in place of רביבים, but it is quite possible that they did not understand the not very common poetic word, and were of opinion that כבישים, which brings out a strong contrast to the lion of the next verse, should be read instead. This is a less forced explanation than that which makes them fail to understand the word and consequently resolve to render it by another which, like it, signifies a multitude: for ἄρνες, in itself, has not that signification. Aq. has ὡς ψεκάδες ἐπὶ πόαν: Symm. ὡσεὶ νιφετός ἐπὶ χόρτον. All the Verss. insert the copula before כרב': in Micah's Heb. such a copula is frequently omitted. The variation of the LXX ὅπως μὴ συναχθῇ μηδεὶς μηδὲ ὑποστῇ ἐν υἱοῖς ἀνθρώπων from the Heb. is explained partly by the mistranslation just touched on and partly by the different vocalization of יקוה: taken as יְקַוֶּה, συναχθῇ translates it: vocalizing and rendering thus they were compelled to read איש for לאיש. In this clause also the Targ. and Pesh. show their relationship: the plu. לבני־אדם is in both represented by the indefinite singular.

V. 7. No alteration.

The Pesh. is only to be accounted for by supposing with Sebök that גבֿן should be read for גבן.* It is the only Vers. which has sing. for the plu. עדרי: this may be

---

* Rich, Eg. and Add. all read as the text: the last of them ha suffered from water at this place, and the text was afterwards inked over.

designed, seeing that it uses the plu. for צאן. *a* and *r* have 'י דבית against 'די of *b*, rightly, no doubt, as in v. 6.

The LXX, Targ. and Vulg. make the apodosis of the second half of the verse begin at ואין: the Pesh. at וטרף; Vulg. and Pesh. mark this by omitting in each case the ו. *Ceperit* is a weak rendering of טרף, but it is found in other passages, such as Hosea v. 14, vi. 1. The LXX ὃν τρόπον is a mistaken resolution of the meaning of אשר but does not oblige us to conjecture כאשר: διαστέλλω also is a poor rendering of רמס, if it be indeed a rendering thereof, and not rather of some other verb substituted for it. The Polyg. rendering of the Pesh., "qui cum decreverit ac deliberaverit praedatur," is very misleading; the true sense of the word is, "who when he departs and mutilates, devours the prey."

V. 8. No alteration.

Ryssel thinks תקוף of *r* against תתקף of *a* and *b* is imper., introduced later for the sake of conformity with M. T. But די is usually fem. and would, therefore, require תְּקֳפִי. It is more likely that the reading in *r* is a mere error of transcription. The Targ. has represented the figurative "be lifted up" by the literal "be strong," and has inserted "O Israel," to make the reference clear. All the Verss. have treated the apocopated תרם as indic. See Gesen. § 72, Rem. 4.

V. 9. No alteration.

B has τοὺς ἵππους ἐκ μέσου σου: A, Ar. and Jer. τοὺς ἵππους σου ἐκ μ. σ. The σου dropped out of B

owing to the presence of so many ους and σου in the immediate context. For סוסיך and מרכבתיך the Targ. has סוסות עממיא and רתיכיהון. Jerome, giving an account of the Jewish explanation current in his day says :—
"Non quod equos et quadrigas tunc habuerit Israel, sed Assyriorum equos et quadrigas, quae in medio urbium tuarum versantur." They could not understand how what looked like a threatening against the people should immediately follow a promise.

V. 10. No alteration.

r omitting קרוי, which undoubtedly is original, shows the difficulty to which the Targumists were reduced by tne procedure mentioned above. They had been unable to get rid of the 2nd pers. suff. pron. in ארצך and consequently had the absurd idea that there were cities of the peoples in the land of Israel; if "cities" were omitted all would be smooth, and consequently *r* drops קרוי. It is a pity that *arces*, used in the Polyg. as the rendering of כרכיהון, has not also been employed instead of *urbes* for the cognate word in the Pesh. Not only is it more suitable in itself, but also it would mark the connection between the Verss.

V. 11. No alteration.

τὰ φάρμακά σου for כשפים does not necessarily imply the reading כשפיך; the pron. may be supplied; the Ar. has no pron. Nor can we adopt the plu. מידיך of the LXX, ἐκ τῶν χειρῶν σου, which the Pesh. followed: at Num. xxii. 7 we have קסמים בידם, and there also LXX has ἐν ταῖς χερσὶν αὐτῶν, and Vulg. read בידים: the Heb. writers felt no difficulty in using a sing. in such cases. Targ. and Pesh. have taken the two words כש׳ and מעוננים as meaning persons: Vulg. has rendered both as meaning practices, *maleficia, divinationes;* each influenced by the wish to secure perfect parallelism: the Targ. consequently found מידך unsuitable and substituted מבינך. It is to be observed, too, that the Vulg. has thus been led to depart from its usual manner of treating מעוננים, which in most other passages it renders by words which signify persons rather than actions. Jerome's "qui loquuntur" for ἀποφθεγγόμενοι is a somewhat colourless translation. But the variety in the LXX renderings of מענ׳ shows that they themselves were not sure of its precise equivalent: we find, for example, κληδονίζεσθαι, οἰώνισμα, ὀρνιθοσκοπέω. For the first word of the pair the Pesh. has the cognate form with the Targ. חרשין, for the second ܟܣܘ݈, from the Greek ζάκορος: it inserts ܬܘܒ in the second half of the verse to bring out the sense and because עוד is actually found in the corresponding clause of the next verse.

Vv. 12, 13. These should be read as one verse as follows:— וְהִכְרַתִּי פְסִילֶיךָ וּמַצֵּבוֹתֶיךָ וְנָתַשְׁתִּי אֲשֵׁרֶיךָ מִקִּרְבֶּךָ וְלֹא־תִשְׁתַּחֲוֶה עוֹד לְמַעֲשֵׂה יָדֶיךָ:

V. 12. As in v. 9, the Targ. for פסיליך and מצבותיך has צלמי עממיא and קמתהון: it avoids the idea of idol-worship, or at all events only allows it to be faintly indicated, by using תשתעבד for תשתחוה: here, as elsewhere, קמ׳ in it represents מצבה; but the Pesh., which agrees with it in other places, in this has ܢܘܒܚ: to explain the Pesh. it is not enough to say that they translated the Heb. word in accordance with the context; they must have mistaken it for מִזְבֵּחַ, and for this have given the inexact rendering which we here find, "burnt-offering," in place of the altar on which the burnt-offering was presented. Passages like Deut. iv. 28 and Ps. cxv. 4, where idols are termed מעשה ידי אדם, and the LXX uses the plu., show that we need not think of a Heb. plu. corresponding to its ἔργοις here: of the other Verss. only the Pesh. has sing. It is curious that the Targ. has the sing. יד.

V. 13. The Vulg. *evellam* is a better representative of נתשתי than the LXX ἐκκόψω. B, Ar. and Jer. have τὰ ἄλση; A adds σου; this illustrates what was said on v. 11. The Ar. repetition of النصبات from v. 12 must be a blunder: at Micah iii. 12 الغاب is the rendering of τὸ ἄλσος. The Targ. again brings in the other nations, שתילי עממיא: here and at Deut. xvi. 21 the Pesh. employs the cognate word to the Targ., but at Isa. xvii. 8, xxvii. 9, where the LXX has δένδρον, it uses ܐܝܠܢ. The final words of the verse are not easy to deal with. We have had והכרתי ערי ארצך in a perfectly natural connection in v. 10 and do not now look for והשמדתי עריך in this unsuitable position. Yet all the Verss., with the possible exception of the Targ., which either read 'צ for 'ע or took 'ע in the sense of 'צ, support the M. T. It has been suggested that we must either change to 'צ or translate 'ע, according to the Aramaic, by "foes." As to the former of these alternatives it would seem that we do not want the transition to v. 14 which would thus be effected, but if anything is required it is a parallel to the first clause of the present verse. As to the latter it is hardly likely that עַר would be found in its Aramaic sense in this verse after being employed in its customary Heb. sense in v. 10. Moreover the passages where עַר has been supposed to mean "enemy" are all doubtful either in meaning or in text. For עָרְךָ, 1 Sam. xxviii. 16, the LXX is μετὰ τοῦ πλησίον σου, as though they read עִם־רֵעֶךָ, which, as Driver says, "is accepted by most moderns," though Wellhausen is inclined to think the M. T. right. At Ps. cxxxix. 20, another of the passages adduced, Ewald, with some MS. authority, reads עָדֶיךָ (or עֲדָתִיךָ). But even if עָרֶיךָ should stand and be rendered "thy enemies" it would not be a parallel case to ours. Delitzsch and von Lengerke hold that it has this meaning, but they support it on the ground that the Psalm contains other Aramaic forms, and Driver says that the verse is probably corrupt. Delitzsch rightly rejects the various proposed alterations of עָרִים at Isa. xiv. 21, עָדִים, עָרִיצִים, עַיִים, as well as the idea of its identity in meaning with צָרִים: to "fill the face of the world with cities" is quite satisfactory. Dan. iv. 16 needs no discussion; the Aram. form is to be expected there. If we are compelled to retain this clause we cannot adopt עֲרָרִיךְ or יְעָרִיךְ in place of עָרֶיךָ: either of these would suppose ἄλση to be a correct rendering of אֲשֵׁרִים. The choice would lie between עַמּוּדֶיךָ, which does not appear elsewhere in place of חַמָּנִים but might fairly serve in its place, and עֲצַבֶּיךָ, which Steiner points out is parallel to

אֲשֵׁרָיו at 2 Chron. xxiv. 18. But I believe that the text is altogether corrupt and that verses 12 and 13 originally formed one longer verse consisting of three clauses: "And I will cut off thy graven images and thy standing images, and I will pluck up thy Asherim out of the midst of thee, and thou shalt no more worship the work of thine hands." Steiner has formed the same conjecture, but I was unaware of this when it occurred to me: his words are, "עָרֶיךָ scheint durch blosses Versehen aus v. 10 hier eingedrungen zu sein."

V. 14. No alteration.

To avoid ascribing unqualified vengeance to God the Targ. rendered נקם by פורגנות דין: the ית, not found in *r*, looks like a later strengthening. The Vulg., "in *omnibus* gentibus", or "in *cunctis* g.", as the Comm. has it, is merely to make plain the fact that it is foreign nations which are meant. The Pesh. and Vulg. treat אשר as plu., referring to אף and חמה, an impossible reference, the object of the verb being the sing. נקם: the LXX renders אשר by ἀνθ' ὧν, but A, not followed by Ar., felt that this left the clause deficient and therefore added μου as object to εἰσήκουσαν: from a like feeling comes the Targ.: "Eo quod haud doctrinam Legis susceperint."

The vocabulary of the Pesh. in the last verses of this chapter is singularly poor: it uses כּ‍ֽ‍ן not only for אבד but twice for הכרית and once for נתש, the latter word in particular being thus most inadequately rendered.

CHAPTER VI.

V. 1. No alteration.

Two Greek renderings of the first clause were current, 'Ακ. δὴ λόγον κυρίου, and 'Ακ. δὴ ἃ ὁ κ. εἶπεν.* These have coalesced, but not so completely as to hide the marks of their juncture, the 'Ακ. δὴ λόγον κύριος κύριος εἶπεν of B betraying it in the repetition of κύριος, and the 'Ακ. δὴ λ. κυρίου ἃ ὁ κ. εἶπεν of A showing it in the plu. relative ἃ, referring to the sing. noun λόγον. The Ar. has simply "Audite nunc quid dixerit Dominus," and in this follows the Pesh. The Vulg. "Audite quae D. loquitur" agrees with Jerome's LXX in taking no note of נָא. From Jerome's having distinguished the LXX by using "loquutus est" it would appear that the Vulg., like the M. T. and the Targ., vocalized אָמַר, whereas the LXX, with which the Pesh. agrees, read אֲמַר. If we are justified, as we certainly seem to be, in thinking that the Pesh. has influenced the Ar. of this verse more powerfully than the LXX has, this will be in favour of the Polyg. ܡܢ ܗܢܐ as against the ܒܗ of Barhebraeus, for the Ar. is ܒܗ: in

---

* "O'. ἀκ. δὴ λ. κ. κ. εἶπεν. Alia exempl. ἀκ. δὴ ἃ ὁ κ. εἶπεν. Sic 23, 42, 49, alii, Hieron., Syro-hex. Parsons e marg. Cod. 86 exscripsit: Ἀ ὁ κ. εἶπεν, ἀκ. δὴ λ.κ. Sed revera hic codex in textu legit: ἀκ. δὴ ἃ ὁ κ. εἶπεν; in marg. autem: ἀκ. δὴ λ.κ."—*Field.*

place of the את which is thus translated Hitzig and Steiner would put אל, the former because a better sense is so obtained, the latter adding that πρὸς of the LXX and *adversum* of Jer. support this: their arguments are not without force, but the change is not absolutely necessary, so far as the Heb. is concerned, and the Verss. allow themselves so much freedom in handling the particles as to make great caution necessary in arguing from them. A inserts καὶ before κριθητι, and the same codex puts οἱ before βουνοὶ in order to approach the Heb. more nearly. There are several various readings to the Targ.: *b* דון, *r* דין, *a* אתוכח; the last of these is from the next verse, and between *b* and *r* it is neither possible nor needful to decide; either would be correct, although this is not one of the verbs usually treated as Med. ': for טוריא of *b* and *r*, *a* has אבהתא, and in this is supported by Kimchi: very likely this is old and was later supplanted by the literal rendering: the same remark would, of course, apply to אמהתא of *a* in place of רמתא, unless it were held that the similarity of form in the last named words led to the reading אמהתא by mistake, and the consequent substitution of 'אב for 'טו in the parallel clause; it is, however, most probable that 'אב and 'אמ are original.

V. 2. No alteration.

הרים. "Der Cod. Vaticanus hat (wie auch Hab. iii. 10 λαοί für הרים in allen LXX-Handschriften steht), λαοί statt ὄρη." So Ryssel. But the Polyg. and Tischendorf's editions represent B as having ὄρη and A βουνοὶ, and although the text of Jerome's translation of the LXX has "montes," the Comments* show that he read βουνοί. The Ar. clearly had λαοί. This can hardly have been other than an intentional resolving of the figurative into the literal, similar, in effect at least, to those various readings of the Targ. on the previous verse discussed above, and originating partly in the λαός μου of v. 3: a people is in question; peoples, therefore, shall listen and judge.

איתן, being so often employed in connection with water-courses, and evidently signifying here something that lies comparatively low, the LXX have rendered φάραγγες and the Ar. has "wadis." "Symmachus et Theodotio transtulerunt, *et antiqua fundamenta terrae*. Quinta autem Editio ipsum Hebraicum posuit, ETHANIM, fundamenta terrae." Jer. *in loc*. The Quinta here is like the LXX at Ps. lxxiv. 15, which gives ἠθάμ. The Pesh. makes ריב a verb, parallel to יתוכח. *a* of Targ. has סדר דינא where the סדר is probably a later addition. For עקריא מיסודי ארעא Kimchi (in Levy) has עק׳ יסודי א׳.

V. 3. No alteration.

הלאתיך. The LXX have two renderings of this word, τί ἐλύπησά σε, ἢ τί παρηνώχλησά σοι. It is easy to understand how a correction of the original τί ἐλ. σε would be put in the marg. and afterwards find its way

---

* "Pro montibus ad quos propheta loquitur; et pro fortibus fundamentis terrae, *colles et valles* LXX transtulerunt, id, ut mihi videtur, intelligentes, quod populus nihil dignum montium auditione fecerit, sed vel collibus qui inferiores sunt a sublimitate montium vel vallibus in ima demersis."

into the text, when we remember the variety of renderings which the Hiph. and Niph. forms of לאה occasioned: sometimes paraphrase is resorted to as though the word were not clearly understood. Jer. is wrong in obelizing τί ἐλ. σε (after Origen) and saying that it is not in the Heb. It would be strange if the attempt were made to replace the more exact παρηνώχ. by the less.* The paraphrase of the first question in the Targ. is a mistaken one: "What good thing have I promised to do to thee, and have not done it?" The Pesh. ܐܣܗܕܘܒܝ is wrongly translated in the Polyg., "produc mihi testes": it should be like the precisely equivalent Targ. אסהד בי, "testimonium perhibe in me." Neither of these Verss. read otherwise than our ענה, for although in other passages the Hiph. of עוד is thus rendered by the Pesh., יענה at Job. xvi. 8 is, in the Targ., אקים לאסהדא : in this passage of Micah also they both are giving what they deemed the sense of ענה.

V. 4. No alteration.

The LXX closely follows M. T. So the Vulg., except that it makes this an ironical question in continuation of the foregoing, something like the irony of St. Paul's, "Forgive me this wrong." Pesh. makes it a question, but not ironical, "Did I not bring thee up &c." Targ. expounds: "misique ante te tres prophetas, Moysen ut doceret judiciorum traditionem, Aharon ut expiaret populum, et Mariam ut instruet mulieres." נבײ of r can hardly be

---

* Jerome improves on the "quid molestus fui tibi?" by "vel ut significantius in Hebraico scriptum est: quo labore te pressi?" Cf. *quae laboraverat*, iv. 7.

correct; נביין of *a* and *b* is wanted. Either "servitutis" of Cod. Amiat., or "servientium" of Sixtine and Comm. is correct, and it is impossible to decide which is original.

V. 5. Probably וּמֶה־עָשִׂיתִי מִן הַשִּׁטִּים עַד־הַגִּלְגָּל.

The Pesh. follows LXX in adding κατὰ σοῦ, and this has made its way into the Vulg. text as given in the Comm. but not into the Sixtine or Cod. Amiat.

מן השטים עד־הגלגל. In one or other form all the Verss. reproduce these words. The Pesh. differs only from M. T. in having o before ܒܓܠ. The Vulg. is precisely the same as the Heb. The LXX has ἀπὸ τῶν σχοίνων ἕως τοῦ Γαλγάλ. Jerome's note on the LXX and the other Greek Verss. runs:—"ubi LXX Schœnis: omnes ipsum Hebraicum SETTIM transtulerunt. . . Unde arbitror et LXX σχῖνον interpretatos esse, hoc est, *lentiscum*: sed paulatim librariorum errore factum esse ut σχοῖνοι, id est, funes, pro σχίνοις, id est, *lentiscis* legerentur." To this may be added that at Joel iii. 18, Targ., Pesh. and LXX render as here, and Jerome, who has *torrentem spinarum* in the Vulg., explains as here; Symmachus, he says, has *vallem spinarum*. The expansion which is found in the Targ.: "Nonne egregia facinora edita sunt in vestri gratiam a convalle Sittim usque ad domum Galgalæ?" introduces us to the consideration of the difficulty which has always been felt to inhere in this fragmentary clause. Jerome shows us that the Jews of his day felt it:—"Ita exponunt: ab eo tempore quo fornicatis estis in Madian usque ad tempus quo Saul apud Galgal est unctus in regem, repetite memoria quae mala operati estis, et quanta bona vobis fecerim &c." His own explanation is as little fitted to meet the requirements either of this verse or of the history :—" De Settim usque ad Galgal, totum exercitum Israel oculis lustrans, et mutans loca." Ewald held that these words were a marginal note intended to mark the portion of the Pentateuch to which the Balaam episode belongs, but there is force in the objection against this that if we omit them from the text we lack a clause corresponding to למען וגו׳, and it is also to be observed that the name of this Parashah is "Balak," or (according to the B. bathra, 14 b., quoted in Levy, Chaldäisches Wörterbuch, II. 304), "Balaam," besides which the Balaam episode did not occur between Shittim and Gilgal. Yet it seems to me incredible that these words should depend on the so far distant זכר־נא, and Maurer's suggestion that ואת אשר עשיתו or ומה־עשיתי has fallen out before מן הש׳ וגו׳ is the best yet made. Of the alternatives ומה ע׳ is to be preferred, to correspond with מה־יעץ. Steiner's view is essentially the same: he points out that Shittim was the last station of the Israelites in the land of Moab, and Gilgal the first in Canaan; he would, therefore, insert עברך, depending on זכר־נא, and indicating God's graciousness displayed all through the passage into the promised land. A moment's attention is due to the Ar. of this verse compared with that of Joel iii. 18: in the Polgy. text of Micah الجبال is found, and it is properly translated *montium*; at Joel iii. 18 الحبال, which is as properly rendered *funium*; there can be no question that the diacritical point has been wrongly affixed in our passage and that in it, as in Joel, we should have الحبال.

The indefinite לְמַעַן דַּעַת has been variously rendered: the LXX ὅπως γνωσθῇ; the Targ. לְמִדַּע; the Pesh. "because he (i.e. Balaam) knew;" the Vulg. "ut cognosceres," which is mistakenly altered into "cognosceret" in Cod. Amiat., the Comm. agreeing with the Sixtine. It is very surprising to find Ryssel asserting that the reason why the LXX (followed by the Pesh.) have δικαιοσύνη for צִדְקוֹת is that the plu. of δικ. is not Greek: "vielmehr ist der Grund einfach der, dass der plural von δικαιοσύνη ungriechish wäre." To say nothing of the frequently occurring plurals of abstract nouns in Greek writers generally we have the plu. of this noun frequently in the Old Testament (*see* Judges v. 11, Ezek. iii. 20, xxxiii. 13, 1 Sam. xii. 7 A). The simple explanation is that they chose to mention the quality instead of naming the actions in which that quality is manifested. Jer. remarks that Symm. uses ἐλεημοσύνας: on the interchange of the two words there is an excellent note in Hatch, p. 49.

V. 6. No alteration.

The Targ. paraphrases the somewhat uncommon אֱלֹהֵי מָרוֹם by "The God whose glory (Shechinah) is in the nigh heavens." The LXX, very strangely and unsuitably, pointed אֱלֹהַי, Θεοῦ μου ὑψίστου. The Pi. of קדם, here rendered καταλαμβάνω, is more often represented by προφθάνω, but in Ps. lxxix. 8, it is προκαταλαβέτωσαν. All the other Verss. clearly have the same reading though they treat it diversely, the Pesh. having the same word as the Heb., the Targ. פלח, and the Vulg. *offeram*. The next verb אכף takes a shade of meaning somewhat removed from its usual one: in the Psalms it commonly signifies to be bowed down or humiliated. It is probably this which has caused the LXX, not quite sure how to turn it here, to use ἀντιλήψομαι, which brings it into connection with the foregoing; they may also, as Ryssel is inclined to think, have wrongly derived the word from כף, and had in mind the suppliant's outstretched hand. The Vulg. "curvabo genu," and the Targ. אשתעבד come nearest the true sense of the word: the Pesh. ܐܒܥ; is a rendering *ad sensum*. Jerome's LXX read εἰ ἀντιλ., beginning this clause like the following ones. The Pesh. and the Ar. bring out the second clause into greater independence by translating as though it opened with ו. Similarly the Pesh. marks the final clause more distinctly as an alternative one by prefixing ܐܘ: to ܩܒܥ, it adds ܐܟܠܐ, probably to balance the descriptive בני שנה added to עג'.

V. 7. No alteration.

It is not easy to decide what the LXX, closely followed by the Vulg., read for נחלי־שמן. B has χιμάρων πιόνων, and A, possibly through a copyist's mistake, ἀρνῶν. If χιμ. is original it must be a translation of עלי'. But it has been suggested that the genuine word is χειμάρρων, from נחלי. To this it is objected that πίονος must in that case have followed and afterwards been altered into the plu. Yet it is more likely that the adjec. has undergone this change than that the LXX found or imagined any other word than נחלי. A stronger argument in favour of the present text of the LXX is that neither Jer. nor the Ar. show any trace of χειμ. But Aq. has χειμ. and

Symm. ῥεῖθρα. On the whole it is fairly certain that the LXX text is corrupt; χιμ. is an error of spelling and χειμ. should be restored; κριῶν, in the first clause, contributed to the mistake. The Targ. agrees with M. T. The Polyg. text of the Pesh., ܟ݁ܪ݂ܒ݁ܘܬ݂ܐ ܕ݁ܡ̈ܝܐ ܕ݁ܬ݂ܘ̈ܪܐ, wrongly rendered "myriadibus armenti juvencarum," means "ten thousands of the strength of cows," "ten thousands of strong cows." But it is a corruption, and Roorda restores ܕ݁ܡܐ̈ ܐܠܦܝ݂. The LXX pointed בְּכוֹרִי, making this clause convey a slightly different idea from that in the next one rather than another expression of it: they also have no μου after ἀσεβείας, but it does not follow that the י in פִּשְׁעִי was not read; μου is used three times in the verse and might be left to be supplied here. Ryssel says that the Vat. and Alex. LXX omit ὑπέρ before ἀσεβ.: Tischendorf's edition and the Polyg. represent B as containing and A as omitting it. Jerome's LXX has ὑπέρ: the omission in A accounts for the Ar., "Facere (i. e. sacrificare) primogenitos meos et fructum ventris mei pro peccato animae meae, impium esset." The Pesh. differs from the Ar. in having two precisely parallel clauses, "Si offeram primogenitum meum, crimini mihi est; si fructus ventris mei, peccato sunt animae meae."

V. 8. No alteration.

Neither Jer. nor the Ar. render the LXX as a question, but our principal texts begin with εἰ: "εἰ ἀνηγγέλη σοι. Alia Exempl. ἀνηγγέλη σόι." Field; r of the Targ. has אִיתְחֲוָה, which agrees with the LXX in being passive, but is without εἰ, whereas a and b have the question, and the active verb היחוה. In both cases the forms without the interrogative particle are probably original: the assertions have been turned into questions for the sake of conformity with v. 7. The Pesh. is followed by the Ar. and the Vulg. in reading אגיד, but the M. T. is better. After the questions which have been put a direct answer by the prophet would have been more fitly introduced by אני, like the "*Ego* respondebo tibi" of Jerome's note. LXX ἀνηγγέλη and Targ. איתחוה do not oblige us to read הֻגַּד: it is common enough for the indefinite 3rd pers. active to bear the sense of *on dit*: LXX and Targ. may have taken it thus, and in so elevated a passage the passive, "it was declared," is too jejune to allow of our believing it to be original. Aq. and Theod. have ἐρρέθη, but Symm. has εἶπε. The Pesh. runs the two first clauses into one, "Indicabo tibi homo quid prosit, quid requirat a te Dominus," feeling that a question concerning Jahweh's requirements would come in awkwardly after the declaration "Indicabo tibi." This has necessitated the omission of ו before מה and of כי־אם immediately after. The Vulg. agrees with it in part, "Indicabo .... quid sit bonum, et quid D. quaerat* a te: utique &c." These changes are additional arguments against the 1st pers. of the verb, the use of which has occasioned them. It is to be observed, also, that the Pesh. gives to טוב here the sense "helpful, profitable," influenced by v. 7.

עשות משפט ואהבת חסד is paraphrased by the Targ. למעבד דין דקשוט ולמרחם גמילות חסדא and it seems

---

* So Cod. Amiat. and Comm.: probably original, the "requirat" of the Sixtine text was adopted because it seemed less anthropopathic.

to regard the next words as the consequence of these, והוי צניע להלכא בדחלתא אלהך, where, like the Pesh. "ad sequendum Deum tuum," it avoids the bolder expression "walk *with* thy God." The Hif. הצנע occurs only here and the Kal only at Prov. xi. 2 : this will partly account for the varieties in the treatment of it. The Targ., as has just been shown, uses the passive partic. Peal צניע, or, as Raschi and Kimchi (in Levy), צנוע. The Pesh. follows the LXX ἕτοιμον εἶναι. "Verbum EsnE, quod LXX transtulerunt *paratum esse*, et nos diximus, *solicitum ambulare*; Theodotio significantius expressit, καὶ ἀσφαλίζου τοῦ πορεύεσθαι μετὰ 'Ελωαίχ . . . . sive ut Quinta Editio transtulit : καὶ φροντίζειν." Jer. *in loc.* Vollers, defending the ἕτ. εἶναι of LXX, finds fault with their rendering ταπεινός at Prov. xi. 2, and Schnurrer would make "Arrogantiam sequitur ignominia, sapientes vero sunt qui probe se exercent" the rendering of בא זדון ויבא קלון ואת־צנועים חכמה. But the LXX, though somewhat paraphrastic, is better, οὗ ἐὰν εἰσέλθῃ ὕβρις, ἐκεῖ καὶ ἀτιμία· στόμα δὲ ταπεινῶν μελετᾷ σοφίαν. A and Ar. have "*The Lord* thy God." See on iv. 5.

V. 9. For וְתוּשִׁיָּה יִרְאֶה שְׁמֶךָ read וְתוּשִׁיָּה לְיִרְאֵי שְׁמוֹ. The LXX, after the model of such passages as Isa. xliii. 7, πάντας ὅσοι ἐπικέκληνται τῷ ὀνόματί μου has φωνὴ κ. τῇ π. ἐπικληθήσεται. None of the other Verss. take the same view : these passages where the Niph. is used are not real analogies to ours, and φωνή cannot be treated like ὄνομα. The Targ. avoids anthropomorphic expressions : "Voce Prophetae D. ad civitatem clamant."

If ותשויה יראה שמך is to stand it can only be by our agreeing with Ewald in taking יראה as the inf., ִ being weaked into ְ: he admits (§ 173) that such a weakening is rare, and to me it seems that the ambiguity and the certainty of misunderstanding the sentence so formed makes the acceptance of it impossible. Ryssel says that the parallel שמעו is a guarantee of the correctness of יראה. But יֵשׁ׳ would require תראה! To turn to the Verss. The LXX has καὶ σώσει φοβουμένους τὸ ὄνομα αὐτοῦ where φωνή is the subject to the verb, as it is in the Pesh., although the latter takes תֻשׁ׳ in a different sense, " vox D. super urbem doctrinam praedicat reverentibus nomen ejus." The Targ. again varies from both these, but has the "fear" idea in common with them and uses the word מלפיא which is cognate to that in the Pesh., " Et doctores timent nomen." The Vulg. agrees with the LXX in its interpretation of תֻשׁ׳ but differs from it, as well as from Targ. and Pesh., in having the suffix pron. of the sec. pers., like the M. T., "Et salus erit timentibus nomen tuum." The simplest account of the whole is that the text originally ran ותושיה לְיִרְאֵי שְׁמוֹ and that the confusion originated in the loss of the ל. The suffix of the third pers. is supported by all except the Vulg.: שמא of the Targ. could only mean God's name, and refers to the third pers. יהוה mentioned just before. As the text is thus not unnaturally accounted for, so also is a more Scriptural idea obtained than that of the M. T.: "to see God's name" is scarcely Biblical; "to fear God's name" is fully so; אז נדברו יראי יהוה, Mal. iii. 16. Nothing need be said respecting Keil's attempt to retain the M. T. by taking "Thy Name" as subject, "Thy Name sees wisdom"!

For שמעו מטה ומי יעדה the Targ. has שמע מלכא ושלטונא ושאר עמא דארעא, where מלכא and שלט' are a double rendering of מטה, the rod being regarded as meaning the ruling powers, of whose sovereignty it is the symbol: וש' ע' דאר' is from a corruption of ומי יעדה, possibly וּמֵעֲדָה. The Pesh. has "Audi O Tribus eum qui contestatur," as if from מִי יָעִיד. The Vulg. has "Audite tribus, et quis approbabit illud": it is peculiar in having the plurals and in taking the ה as suffix. The verb implied in *approbabit* is probably the same as the Pesh. thought of: in the Comm. we have "Audite decem tribus Samariae, quae vobis Dom. contestatur: adhuc ignis &c.," where "quae v. D. contestatur" seems to be another way of putting the idea "Et quis approb. illud?" The LXX takes עוד, which in the M. T. and the remaining Verss. stands at the head of the next verse, as belonging to this, but it reads עיר, ἄκουε φυλή, καὶ τίς (A τί, a copyist's blunder) κοσμήσει πόλιν*; The sense thus obtained and that conveyed by the following sentences in the LXX do not justify us in forsaking the M. T. and the remaining Verss., either as to the division of the verses or as to the change to עיר. On the other hand we cannot follow the Pesh. or Vulg. The former, with Targ. and LXX, has made שמעו sing. to agree with מטה: the Vulg., unable to see the propriety of one tribe being thus addressed, especially when its Heb. text had שמעו, has

---

* The Ar., by mistake, read πολύ.—*Ryssel*.

made מטה plu. They were all misled by their initial error, the taking מטה as a vocative; it is the object to the verb, and the explanation of the fem. suffix—מטה being a masc. noun—is that the noun is used in the figurative sense of punishment or calamity and that the reference to it in the suffix is quite general and indefinite: in such cases the fem. is common.

V. 10. No alteration.

אש cannot be taken otherwise than as the Aramaic form equivalent to יש, found also at 2 Sam. xiv. 19. The translation by "fire" in LXX, Pesh and Vulg., in no case produces a satisfactory meaning. The LXX makes the verse an ironical question in continuation of τίς κος. κ.τ.λ.: μὴ πῦρ καὶ οἶκος ἀνόμου * θησαυρίζων θησαυροὺς ἀνόμους † καὶ μετὰ ὕβρεως ἀδικίας ‡. After its μὴ π., the LXX was compelled to insert καὶ: the θησαυρίζων is also put in to make sense. Roorda's conjecture that μέτρα should be read for μετὰ is borne out by Amos viii. 5, where איפה is rendered μέτρον: for רזון they thought of זדון, which is rendered ὕβρις, Prov. xi. 2: זעמה is translated ἀδικίας because the ἀδ. is the cause of the curse. The Ar. translates the Greek almost literally, and it is quite misleading on the part of

---

* A and Ar. ἀνόμων, either a transcriber's error or an alteration to suit the other plurals: Jer. agrees with B.

† A and Ar. ἀνομίας, a correction to accord with Heb.: Jer. supports B.

‡ A ἀδικία, a correction to produce a better sense: Jer. and Ar. agree with B.

the Polyg. to punctuate: "non ignis. At domus, &c."
The Pesh. takes the entire verse to be the testimony
mentioned in the foregoing one: "Adhuc ignem esse in
domo scelerati, horrea iniquitatis, et mensuram parvam
dolosam." The incongruousness of the "fire" idea comes
out more glaringly here than in the LXX: before "house"
it, with Vulg., supplies "in:" it feels the awkwardness of
the asyndeton and therefore interpolates "and" before
"treasures:" its "dolosam" is partly due to the influence
of the LXX, the word זְעוּמָה not being a very common
one: in v. 12, where LXX have ἀσεβείας, it uses the same
word as here. The Targ. ingeniously escapes all difficulties by ending the question at רָשָׁע and making the
rest a predicate: "Numquid adhuc extat domus impii?
thesauri impietatis et mensurae iniquitatis adducunt male-
dictionem." The Vulg., "mensura minor irae plena,"
answers very well to זְעוּמָה seeing that זָעַם is several times
rendered *irascor*.

V. 11. No alteration;·but אָזְכֶּה is another form of
יִזְכֶּה.

הַאֶזְכֶּה, as was to be expected, has been a source of perplexity. The LXX,* εἰ δικαιωθήσεται, regarded it as 3rd
pers. sing. Kal and gave it a passive turn, as it does
with so many active verbs. The Targ., according to its
manner, uses the 3rd pers. plu. Peal. The Pesh. unites
the characteristics of these two and has the third pers.

---

* A and Ar. καὶ εἰ κ.τ.λ., a correction to put more force into the
question.

plu. passive, employing הֲאֶזְכֶּה instead of the simple interrogative. The Vulg. has the 1st pers. sing., "justificabo." Ewald regards אִי as similar to the אִשׁ of v. 10, a sharpening of the *yi* sound, א for יְ, introduced because of the tendency of *y* and *i* to flow into each other. Roorda would read אֲזַכֶּה or אֲזֻכֶּה, making the pron. refer to Jerusalem, which is represented by this suffix in the next verse. And Cheyne, also referring to Jerusalem, thinks הֲתִזְכֶּה possible. The choice really seems to lie between Jerome's Hiph., which represents the Divine Being as speaking in the first person*, and Ewald's suggestion. The former of these does nothing to explain the other renderings, and אִי would readily, whether correctly or not, be pointed in the manner which this implies: the Hiph. of זכה is not used elsewhere, to which may be added, with reference to Roorda, that where the Pi. occurs it is in a different sense from the one required here: for this meaning we should rather expect אַצְדִּיק: and, as Roorda perceived, we should look for the object after the Hiph. The Vulg. itself felt the force of this last consideration, as is plain from its leaving בְּ untranslated both times: "Numquid justificabo stateram impiam, et sacelli pondera dolosa?" On the whole Ewald's explanation best recommends itself.

---

* Jennings and Lowe, *Expositor*, Dec. 1885, p. 436, refer with approval to the R. V., "Shall I be pure with wicked balances, &c.?" which would imply the same questioner as in verses 6 and 7. After this questioner has been answered in the eighth verse, and the fresh subject-matter been introduced in v. 9, the recurrence of the same enquirer would seem out of place.

For ἐν ζυγῷ ἄνομος, καὶ ἐν μαρσίππῳ στάθμια δόλου Ryssel is inclined to believe that the LXX originally had ἐν ζ. ἀνομίας, κ. ἐν μ. σταθμίων δ., the ἀνομίας being afterwards altered into ἄνομος to get a definite subject, and the genitive στ. being consequently turned into a nominative. This would admirably restore the balance of the clauses which is lost in our present text. The corruption, however, is of old standing: Jer. and Ar. show no trace of the better reading. The Targ. explains אבני מרמה by מתקלין רברבין ודעדקין. The Pesh. has one of its many Greek words, ܥܠܝ̈ܡܐ.

V. 12. No alteration.

אשר עשיריה מלאו חמס. LXX ἐξ ὧν τὸν πλοῦτον αὐτῶν ἀσεβείας ἔπλησαν. Jer. and Ar. read ἐξ ὧν τ.π. (τῆς?) ἀσεβείας αὐτῶν ἐπ. Tischendorf's note is, "ed. rom. ἔπλησαν; et in fine αὐτῶν." These were attempts to improve the text; the plu. suffix cannot have been read with חמס. Taking the LXX then as given above we see that אשר was referred to the weights &c., of v. 11: the הָ, referring to a subject not yet named, seemed out of place, and so led the translators to think of עשרם instead of עשיריה: the verb was pointed as Piel. The Targ., with the other Verss., read the verb as Kal: "The treasures of whose rich men are filled with violence."* For חמס the Pesh. has ܥܘܠܐ, its word for זעומה in v. 10: elsewhere its treatment of חמס is by no means uniform; we have ܚܛܘܦܝܐ, ܚܒܠܐ and ܩܛܝܪܐ, but after the use of ܥܘܠܐ

---

* So Ryssel correctly as against the Polyg.: "Cujus divites replent thesauros suos rapina."

for 'עי in v. 10 it is only the influence of the LXX, ἀσεβείας, which can account for the unduly mild word here. For רמיה LXX read רמה: the other Verss. rightly follow M.T., as sense and parallelism demand.

V. 13. No alteration.

Baer and Delitzsch's note runs:—"החלתי sine Iod tertiae radicalis in Soncin. sicut in E 3. In E 2. החליתי scriptum erat, sed Iod expunctum." The Targ. regards the word as the first pers. sing. Hiph. of חלה. We find in Jerome's translation of the LXX proof that some MSS. of this Vers. also took it thus, "Et ego cruciavi te perditione propter peccata tua," though curiously enough he comments on this in a manner which implies our present LXX text, and does not appear to note the difference: "Et ego incipiam te percutere perditione p.p. tua." It will be noticed that the former of these renderings leaves out הכותך. The Pesh. and Vulg. agree with the LXX of our common text, καὶ ἐγὼ ἄρξομαι τοῦ πατάξαι σε, a rendering which is partly due to the fact that the suffix pronoun seems wanted with הח', and partly to the influence of such passages as Deut. ii. 25, אָחֵל תֵּ; 31, הַחִלֹּתִי תֵּת. But the suffix with the first verb is not absolutely necessary: at Hosea vii. 5 we have יום מלכנו החלו שרים חמת מיין which is almost exactly similar, where, too, the Verss. (including Targ.) wrongly translate with the LXX ἤρξαντο. And notwithstanding such passages as Deut. ii. 25, it seems much more in accordance with the vigour of this prophecy to find here " I have made thee sick " rather than " I have begun," or " I will begin." The LXX, Targ. and Pesh. make הֲשִׁמֹּם equivalent to a finite verb parallel to הֹח': the Vulg. endeavours to approach nearer to the M. T. by making it subordinate to הֹח': "et ego ergo coepi percutere te perditione propter peccata tua." B commences the second half of the verse with ἀφανιῶ: A and Ar. (which Pesh. agrees with) καὶ ἀφ. The καὶ is probably an insertion made for the purpose of bringing out the grammatical independence of the second declaration. Ar. agrees with B's ἐν ταῖς ἁμαρτίαις as against the ἐπὶ of A.

Baer and Delitzsch's note on the last word of the verse is, "חֹטָאתֶךָ sine Vav et Jod plurali in Soncin. Complut. et plerisque codd. F adnotat לית חסר. Masora parva ms. חסר דחסר, B: חטאתך לית כתיב כן."

V. 14. No alteration.

The Pesh. did not see the force of אתה: the Ar. also neglects the σὺ of the LXX, but does not copy the ὁ with which the Pesh., as in so many other places, begins the clause.

יְשַׁחֲךָ has given much trouble. In the leading uncials of the LXX we find συσκοτάσει or σκοτάσει, as also in Theod. Jer. appears to have been unacquainted with this, for he gives, without remark, "et ejiciam te," and many codices of the LXX * have καὶ ἐξώσω σε, as if from וְאָסַחֲךָ. Aq. has καταφυτεύσω and Symm. διαφθερεῖ. The Targ. renders ישחך בקרבך by ‡ במעך למרע לך ויהי:

---

* "(xii, marg. και σκοτασει) 23, 40, 68, 87, 97, 133, (228 marg. ut Ed.) 233, 240, 310, 311."—*Holmes and Parsons*.

‡ r adds וּמְחָא, a mistaken repetition from v. 13.

the Pesh., with the same meaning, has "dysentery:" both these may come from ישׁח. The Vulg. "humiliatio tua" is evidently a translation of a noun derived from שׁחח. There can be no hesitation in rejecting the LXX "it shall be dark," which implies a transposition of the letters שׁ and ח: the parallelism demands a word which in some way shall refer to emptiness. כחשׁ, Cheyne's suggestion, would explain all the Verss. save the Vulg. and would satisfy the requirements of the context. Yet one hesitates to accept it, because it involves the rejection of a difficult word, ἀπ. λεγ., which accounts for the Verss. and might well bear the meaning required. And there is reason for Hitzig's belief that Simonis is right in deriving ישׁח from وحش: the transposition required is exemplified in many other cases, and the sense which وحش bears, especially in Conj. IV., is quite satisfactory. This is one of the passages where the LXX, ἐν σοί, neglect the force of בקרבך: Aq. and Symm. are more careful, the former having ἐν ἐγκάτῳ σου, the latter εἰς τὰ ἐντός σου. Those MSS. of the LXX which read καὶ ἐκνεύσει* imply the Heb. וְתָסַג or וְתִסֹּג in place of וְתַסֵּג. Jer. † read καταλήψῃ, which he rendered *apprehendes*, the word used in the Vulg.: these, with the Targ. and Aq. (καταλήψῃ), are renderings either of תַשִּׂיג or of the M. T. taken in the sense common to תשׂיג. Symm. has ἕξεις, Theod. ἀνα-

---

* At Judges iv. 18 A has ἔκνευσον for סוּרָה, which might almost lead us to suspect a confusion of ב and ר here.

† So also 23, 40, 68, 87, 97, 130, (228 marg. ut. Ed.) 233, 240, 310, 311, Cyrill. Alex.

ψύξεις. The M. T. accords well with the context and should not be altered. Though the words used in Targ. and Pesh. are not identical the Polyg. translators have *assequeris* for both: *bona* also is wrongly added after the verb in the rendering of the Pesh. None of the other Verss. agree with the distinction which the LXX makes by its διασωθῇς and διασωθῶσιν: from these Verss. it is also impossible to gather that there was any difference in their texts corresponding to the תַּפְלִיט and תְּפַלֵּט of the M. T.: but this difference should be maintained; Hitzig points out that the Hiph. means "to bring into a position of safety," and the Pi. "to save alive," and a better sense is thus made of the passage than that which results if both words are read alike. The Pesh. ܡܦܠܛ is preferable to the Vulg. *quos*, which came in under the influence of the LXX. The LXX alone has avoided ascribing the calamity to God, εἰς ρομφαίαν παραδοθήσονται.

V. 15. No alteration.

תדרך is here rendered πιέσεις. The verbs more frequently used for this process are πατέω and τρυγάω, specially the former. Our translation may be due to a man who was familiar with the pressing rather than the treading of olives. The Targ. has interpolated its usual word for treading before תירוש, and before זית has employed תבדר, *excuties*. For תירוש it has ענבין, thinking it more suitable that the grapes should be trodden than that the must should be. Jerome's LXX is a literal rendering of the M. T., "Et uvam (*uvas* in the comments) et non bibes vinum." But this is certainly an alteration

occasioned by the Heb. The mass of MSS. have καὶ
οἶνον καὶ οὐ μὴ πίητε: the Pesh., somewhat closely following this, has " et vinum exprimes et non bibes :" the Ar.,
more briefly still, " nec bibetis vinum." The origin of
this variation is to be found in the LXX having read
תשתה־יין for תשתיון.

V. 16. For עַמִּי read עַמִּים: possibly for וְיִשְׁתַּמֵּר read
וְיִשְׁמְרוּ.

וישתמר חקות עמרי. Of this there are two renderings
in the LXX; the first, καὶ ἀφανισθήσεται ·νόμιμα * λαοῦ
μου, attached to v. 15; the second, καὶ ἐφύλαξας τὰ
δικαιώματα Ζαμβρί. Jerome's note implies that the latter
is an alternative and improved rendering introduced by
himself or others whom he knew, for the express purpose
of coming nearer to the Heb.: "*Et dissipabuntur legitima
populi mei:* pro quo nos posuimus propter sermonis consequentiam *et custodisti praecepta Amri* licet et in Hebraeo
scriptum sit *et custodita sunt praecepta Amri* . . . . si
enim scriptum esset in Hebraeo AMMI, recte LXX trans-
tulissent, *populi mei:* nunc vero quum scriptum sit AMRI
et RES litera addita, non populi nomem, sed patrem Achab
sonat." To this it is only necessary to add that עמי may
have been read through the influence of the עמי at the
end of this verse, where חרפת עמי is not very unlike in
form to חקות עמי, and that as a verb they most likely

---

* ڡل, by which the Ar. renders this, would be more exactly represented by "cogitatio" than by the "judicium" of the Polyg., which
is too ambiguous.

thought of וישתוממו, השמם in v. 13 being rendered ἀφανιῶ. Turning now to the alternative LXX we find, according to Jer., that the 2nd pers. sing. active ἐφύλαξας has been deliberately used for the sake of conformity with the verbs in the 2nd pers. which have preceded and are to follow, whereas the Heb. text had the 3rd pers. plu. passive. This would imply that we must read the Niph. וְיִשָּׁמְרוּ or else that we must regard the וישתמר, the indef. 3rd pers. sing. which so frequently is used where we employ a passive, as the original, for which וישמרו had been substituted in Jerome's day to make the meaning indisputable. On the whole the latter is perhaps the better explanation, because it is difficult to see how the Massoretes could have been led to introduce so much harder a reading into the text: their reading must have been well supported by tradition. Ewald, § 124, 2, points out that although rarely, and chiefly in late writings, the Hithp. is used passively. The other Verss. do not help us here: Pesh. agrees with LXX ἐφύλ., and Targ. has 2nd pers. plu. active, which may be occasioned by the עבדתוך which comes immediately after. The ועל די of Targ. compared with ܥܠ of Pesh. again indicates the close connection between these Verss. Jer.,* with the Ar., had 'Αμρί instead of our Ζαμβρί: there is no consistency in the LXX treatment of עמרי, as the following list shows:—

---

* The above cited note shows this and is decisive against the Ombri of Cod. Amiat., which no doubt was a later correction.

1 Kings xvi. 16, 21, 25, 30 B has Ἀμβρί, A has Ζαμβρί, and the latter in v. 16 has the same for זמרי.
2 Kings viii. 26 B and A have Ἀμβρί.
1 Chron. vii. 8   „   „   Ἀμαρία.
    „   ix. 4   „   „   Ἀμρί.
    „   xxviii. 18 B has Ἀμβρί, A Ἀμαρί.
    „   viii. 36 ימרה in B is Ζαμβρί and in A Ζαμρί.

On the whole it may perhaps be said that the Z is more favoured by A than by B, the example last given being exceptional in that the Heb. word is not the same. To correspond with בית אחאר the Targ. have put בית before עמרי: in place of "*all* the works" it has put the verb, "ye have done the works": its translator has rightly rendered עובדי by "opera," whereas the cognate word in the Pesh. is too strongly given by "facinora." Jerome's note quoted above entitles us to believe that his departure from M. T. and all the other Verss. in "ambulasti" is only "propter sermonis consequentiam."

Ἐν ταῖς ὁδοῖς αὐτῶν of B for במעצותם is probably a free rendering in harmony with the verb "to walk"; ἐν ταῖς βουλαῖς αὐ. of A and Jer. is a correction according to the Heb. The Targ. "laws" and Pesh. "views" come directly from the Heb., and the latter has had some influence on the Ar. روبانهم. Having used ܘ ܠܟ in place of the simple ו at the beginning of the verse, the Pesh. is now compelled to translate למען as if it were לכן: this Vers. has also altered the suffix of אתך into the 3rd pers. for the sake of conformity with the הָ in ישביה; quite unnecessarily, the people being directly addressed in the first instance and the city thought of in the second. For παραδώ σε, A, by reduplication, has παραδώσω σε, and for *darem te* Cod. Amiat., by a similar mistake, has *darent*. The Targ. here avoids ascribing the calamity to God, precisely as the LXX did in v. 15, using for תתי the perfectly general and impersonal למסר. The לאשתממו by which this version in several passages renders לשרקה is singularly inexact; nowhere does this inexactness come out so strikingly as at Jer. xix. 8, where שמה and שרקה are respectively rendered as here by צדו and אשתממו, but when the verbs ישם וישרק follow, fresh words, יכלי ויניד, have to be found. It is next to impossible that the Ar. third pers. plu. for λήψεσθε can be correct; the diacritical point is wrongly placed. For חרפת the LXX and the Targ. use plurals to bring into view the various items of reproach. Whether we believe, with several critics, that the mark of abbreviation has been lost sight of, or hold that the ם of עמים has been omitted through confusion with the ת* that follows, there cannot be much doubt that the plu. is here intended. It has indeed been said that the thought required by the context is, "the reproach which my people brings on me." But if this were so how could *they* be said to bear it? It would be *He* who bore it. And the threatening, "Ye shall bear the reproach of peoples," is quite in harmony with the tenor of the verse.

---

* Is it by accident that at 2 Sam. xxii. 44, and Ps. cxliv. 2, two of the three passages where the Massora misses ם, the next word begins with ת? At all events we know that these letters were very liable to be mistaken for each other.

CHAPTER VII.

V. 1. No alteration.

The noun אֹסֶף occurs at Isa. xxxii. 10, xxxiii. 4, in both instances in the sing. number. The deviation of the LXX from our M. T., συνάγων for אסף׳, does not carry much weight seeing that the Greek translators have failed to understand the word in both the verses of Isaiah, for אסף בלי יבוא having οὐκέτι μὴ ἔλθῃ, as though this were an example of the well-known idiomatic use of יסף with another verb, and for אסף החסיל, ἐάν τις συναγάγῃ ἀκρίδας, turning the noun into the infin. of the verb. But the Pesh., which proceeds independently of the LXX, as well as the Vulg. which is not independent, read the sing. The combined testimony of the LXX and the Pesh. is not lightly to be set aside, yet one can hardly doubt that the plu. is original and was chosen for the sake of parallelism with עללת, such a use of the plu. being justified either on Hitzig's ground that a number of days would be occupied in the fruit-gathering, or, as Keil prefers, because the saying applies to all such gatherings. The entire clause אללי לי כי הייתי כאספי־קיץ כעללת בציר is rendered Οἴμοι ὅτι ἐγενήθην (A ἐγενόμην) ὡς συνάγων καλάμην ἐν ἀμητῷ καὶ ὡς ἐπιφυλλίδα ἐν τρυγητῷ; this turn being given to the expression because the LXX understood it as the personal plaint of the prophet, an idea which the Targ. brings out with still greater clearness by its rubric, אמר נביא. Ryssel's explanation of καλάμην is founded on the fact that at Isa. xvii. 6 עללת is rendered καλάμη: he thinks that it was so rendered here, the כ being passed over as in the Vulg.*, and that the better translation ἐπιφυλλ. being afterwards substituted the κ. found its present place as though it were for קיץ. There is much to commend this view; the alternative would be that the LXX wished to bring into prominence the thought of fruitless endeavour under the figure of a man gathering straw instead of grain, and accordingly read קש for קיץ. The LXX and the Pesh. make the second member of the comparison more distinct by prefixing "and."

אין אשכול לאכול בכורה אותה נפשי. The majority of our MSS. of the LXX, with which the Ar. agrees, read οὐχ ὑπάρχοντος βότρυος τοῦ φαγεῖν τὰ πρωτόγονα. οἴμοι ψυχη, κ.τ.λ. A few, however, have οὐχ ὑπ. β. τ. φ. τὰ π. ἐπεποθήσεν ἡ ψυχή μου, and Jer., who renders "primitiva, quae passa est anima mea. Vae mihi anima &c," must have had a codex containing this text before him, the ἐπεπονθήσεν in it being a misspelling of ἐπεποθ. and ἆ, which in the other codices of this class may have been lost after πρωτόγονα, being possibly, though not necessarily, found. No doubt these codices have here a correction after the Heb., which was first placed in the margin and afterwards in the text, in Jerome's exemplar without displacing

---

* "Sicut qui colligit in autumno racemos vindemiae:" the two clauses are run together, and קיץ regarded as an adverb of time.

the older rendering. With reference to that older rendering it need only be said that even in the Greek τὰ πρωτ., as object to φαγ. does not come in well after βότρυος; that the other Verss. all support the M. T.; and that אותה has been confounded with אויה (Ps. cxx. 5) or with אוי.

The Targ. contains two renderings of the first half of this verse, the one being an interpretation derived from v. 2 and the other what was deemed a literal translation. The first runs וי לי ארי הויתי כמסף טביא בעדן דאבדו חסידיא מן ארעא. The second הא כסיופי קיטא כעוללן בתר קטוף, where בתר makes the idea of unsatisfactoriness more emphatic, and סיופי is derived from סוף. The second half of the verse is interpreted rather than translated: "Non est vir qui habeat opera bona, bonos (*tamen*) appetit anima mea."

V. 2. No alteration.

The MSS. vary between εὐσεβής of B and εὐλαβής of A and Ar. as the rendering of חסיד. But there are also traces of a totally different word, possibly ἀναστρέψας, having been used. Holmes and Parsons end their note with the words, "revertens a terra.—Origen ii. 357." Origen ii. p. 357 (De La Rue's Edition), in the 23rd Homily on Numbers, runs as follows: "Sed et illa humanum genus lamentantis Dei vox est qua dicitur per prophetam. *Heu me, quoniam factus sum sicut qui congregat stipulam in messe et sicut racemus in vindemia, quia non est spica nec botrus ad edenda primogenita. Hei mihi anima quoniam periit revertens a terra, et qui corrigat in honimibus non est.* Domini sunt istae voces, genus humanum lugentis." In the fifth chapter of the first Homily on Ezekiel Origen quotes the same verse: "*Heu mihi, anima mea, quia periit revertens a terra, et qui corrigat inter homines non est.*"* It is further to be noted that Jer. followed Origen. Martinianay's Edition of the Comm. gives *revertens* both in the text and in the comments: Migne and Vallarsius both give *reverens* in the text and *revertens* in the comments: the Rev. G. M. Youngman informs me that in the only MS. of Jerome's Commentaries which he finds in the British Museum *revertens* appears twice.* For חסיד there must have been a variant הסיר: the very fact that it is not easy to understand how this could be rendered by such a word as ἀναστρέψας will help to account for the almost total disappearance of the latter. Οἴμοι ψ. of v. 1 compelled the LXX to begin this verse with ὅτι.

The Targ. אבדו חסידיא is an instructive illustration of the readiness with which they turned the indefinite sing. into the plu. Κατορθῶν is the rendering of ישר as at Prov. ii. 7, xiv. 11. The לדמים is a sufficient token of the mistakenness of the LXX in reading יריבו for יארבי:

---

* I owe both these references to Origen's Homilies to my friend, the Rev. Ronald Bayne, who most kindly looked up the first of them at my request, and himself discovered the second.

† Mr. Youngman's note runs thus: "Brit. Mus. Reg. 4 C xi. Comm. S. Hier. in Dan. et Proph. Min. Saec. xii.,—

Tristis est anima usque ad mortem periit *revertens* de terra vel antiχρο interficiente scos

Et iterum. Ve mihi anima periit *revertens* a terra et qui corrigat inter homines non est."

the other Verss. read as M. T. "In sanguine" of the Vulg. is so peculiar that we should alter it were there any authority for doing so: in other passages the dative or a preposition and accusative go with *insidior*. The Pesh. neglects to mention the blood: "omnes struent insidias." It is somewhat remarkable that the Pesh. fails to reproduce the plu. דמים in many passages; see Isa. ix. 4, Ezek. xxii. 2, Micah iii. 10, Zech. ix. 7, Ps. v. 7, Prov. i. 18.

איש את־אחיהו יצודו חרם. LXX ἕκαστος τὸν πλησίον αὐτοῦ ἐκθλίβουσιν ἐκθλιβῇ. For יצודו they read יצרו, which is a better parallel to their יריבו, but not so good a one to the true reading יארבו: the other Verss. correctly agree with M. T. In common with the other Verss. the LXX has understood חרם in the same way as at Mal. iii. 24, where והכיתי את־הארץ חרם is rendered καὶ πατάξω τὴν γῆν ἄρδην. Thus taken, it corresponds well with לדמים, and if it had been intended in the sense found at Ezek. xxvi. 5 (σαγηνῶν), xxxii. 3 (ἀγκίστρῳ) we should have looked for the בְ *instrumenti* of Hab. i. 15, יגרהו בחרמו. Aq. and Symm. have θηρεύουσιν ἀναθέματι. τὸν πλησίον is a softening of the very severe "they hunt every man *his brother*," and the Targ., which has slightly enlarged the foregoing clause, "omnes parant insidias sanguinis justi effendendi causa," softens this clause, though not in the same way as LXX, "unusquisque fratrem suum ad exterminium produnt." For מסרין, the reading of *b* and *r*, *a* has מצדין, which cannot be anything but an alteration occasioned by the Heb.

V. 3. For לְהֵיטִיב read הֵיטִיבוּ.

עַל־הָרַע כַּפַּיִם לְהֵיטִיב. Few expressions in the book are treated more diversely than this. The LXX regarded הרע as noun and article, ἐπὶ τὸ κακὸν τὰς χεῖρας αὐτῶν ἑτοιμάζουσιν. Probably its verb was הטיבו: it is true that ἑτοιμ. is most frequently a translation of כון or one of its conjugations, but it might well stand for היטיב here, and the latter verb is so strongly witnessed to by the remaining Verss. that we cannot set it aside. There is no need to suppose that the suffix pron. was read, although all the Verss. agree in employing it. The Vulg. "Malum manuum suarum dicunt bonum" implies the same verb, היטיבו, but seems to rest on the grammatical solecism of treating רע as in the construct state governing כפ': if it had been in that relation the article would have stood before the latter word. The Targ. מבאשין בידיהון ולא מוטיבין is as though their text had been עַל־הָרַע כַּפַּיִם וְלֹא היטיבו, and the Pesh. betrays the influence both of the LXX and the Targ.: "Their hands are good at doing evil, and they do not good." Our choice of text is thus threefold. We may adhere to the M. T. and understand it according to the rule in Gesen. § 132, 3, Rem. 1, "For doing evil," or, "For evil, both hands are ready to do it eagerly." In this case הרע might be either the Hiph. infin. of רעע, or the noun רע with the article. Against this it is to be noted that the other Verss. show no trace of the ל which is thus retained, and further, that the saying is so elliptical as to arouse strong suspicion of its genuineness. We may follow Targ. and Pesh., which have לא or ולא in place of ל and the finite verb like the

LXX. A very good sense is thus obtained, but one doubts whether the contrast would not have been so put as to have the same form, על־הטוב, in the second member as in the first; לא היטיבו as the contrast to על־הרע כפ׳ is not satisfactory. We may follow the LXX, which produces a quite acceptable sense and involves very slight alteration of the text. Moreover, although the Vulg. *interprets* the verb differently, taking it declaratively, it agrees with the LXX in the verb and in the omission of ל. When we remember that the vowel letter ו need not have been written it seems quite possible that the word might be mistaken for inf. const. and ל inserted to win a better sense. Without insisting on the binding necessity of this particular correction it may be looked upon as the likeliest, and it is at all events most probable that the M. T. is corrupt.

השר שאל * והשפט בשלום. The brachyology has proved troublesome. A literal translation is found in the Vulg.: "princeps postulat, et judex in reddendo est," and Jer. explains the last words: "sic alium judicans, quomodo ipse ab alio judicatur, ut praestent sceleribus suis mutuum favorem, et in alterius crimine se defendant." The Targ. read and understood the words in the same way: "princeps postulat, et judex dicit. Fac pro me†, ut retribuam tibi." The Pesh. agrees with the Targ. in

---

* Baer and Delitzsch's note is: "שָׁאָל defective in codd. et edd. veteribus sicut omnibus omnino locis."

† Either the דשלם of *b* or the ואשלם of *a* is more likely to be original than the הא אישלים of *r*.

supplyng אָמַר in the second half: "praefectus postulat *dicens**; Affer: et judex dicit, Da munus." The three Verss. just referred to are equally unanimous in supporting the M. T. of the next clause, the only variations being that Pesh. and Vulg. rightly keep the sing., "desiderium," whereas the Targ., *more suo*, prefers the plu., and that the Targ. (see below) detaches הוּא from this clause. But the brevity of the clause which we have considered above was a stumbling-block to the LXX and it has therefore altered both language and arrangement. For השר ש' והשפט בש' והגדול דבר חות נפשו הוא it has ὁ ἄρχων αἰτεῖ, καὶ ὁ κριτὴς εἰρηνικοὺς λόγους ἐλάλησε, καταθύμιον ψυχῆς αὐτοῦ ἐστίν. For בְּשָׁלוֹם, בַּשָׁלוֹם or לְשָׁלוֹם (as at Gen. xxxvii. 4†) has been read, and הגדול being omitted דבר has been taken as 3rd pers. sing. Pi. The crux has clearly been בשלום, and the LXX has been unable to see that "the prince asks (for gifts) and the judge (judges) for a recompense" may fairly be got from the words as they stand. Their own rendering cannot harmonize with the context, seeing that "peaceful words," unless a crafty purpose were in some way indicated, are no part of the evil conduct here ascribed to the authorities. And if it were replied that the allusion is contained in καταθ. κ.τ.λ. it is indisputable that such an allusion does not lie on the surface. Jer. felt the difficulty of the words

---

* So the Polyg. and Ryssel, regarding the ܘ as introducing the word quoted. But no such ܘ precedes ܪܒܐ, and the better sense would be: "the prince asks for *gold*, &c."

† LXX, λαλεῖν αὐτῷ οὐδὲν εἰρηνικόν.

καταθ. κ.τ.λ. and hardly succeeded in surmounting it when he explained: "Accipit enim munera, desiderium animae suae." Another objection to the LXX is that the partic. דְּבַר corresponds better to the שׁאל at the opening. הוּא, according to Ewald, § 311, 1, *b*, is the separate pron. employed to give emphasis to the suffix in נפשׁו. But Driver's view of it as the pronoun which implies the copula is better, § 198. There is absolutely nothing to recommend the procedure in the Targ. where הוי is read for it, and a sentence made out of this and the next words, וי עליהון על דקלקלוהא.

Both as to the word itself and as to the connection the Verss. vary widely in their treatment of וַיְעַבְּתוּהָ. The Vulg., "et conturbaverunt eam", follows M. T. both in words* and in division. Jerome's explanation of "Eam", "vel urbem, vel veritatem, sive terram de qua supra dicitur, *periit sanctus de terra*", sufficiently shows that *eum* of Cod. Amiat. is a scribe's error. The Targ., in the reading quoted above, divides as the M. T. does, but is a translation of תְּעַב. The LXX καὶ ἐξελοῦμαι τὰ ἀγαθὰ αὐτῶν would require as its original וְאֶעֱוֹת טוּבָם†, taking טוּבָם from the next verse and treating the sing. as a plu. in the same way as it often does with רֵע and טוֹב. The first pers. sing., however, can only be looked on as a conscious correction made in order to harmonize with the following part of the translation. The Pesh. here again agrees with the Targ. in part and the LXX for the rest,

---

* *Conturbo* does not appear to be used for עוּת, and it is therefore permissible to assume that it is the rendering of עבת.

† Or possibly, as Schleusner thinks, וְאַעֲבֵר.

reading תָעֵב and the 3rd pers. plu. of the verb with the former but making טובם the object of the verb with the latter. The Ar. here forsakes the LXX for the Pesh., at all events so far as the *meaning* of the verb is concerned, although it keeps the first pers. sing. Its word is ارذل: at Micah iii. 9, Ps. cxix. 163, the Heb. is תעב, the LXX βδελύσσω, the Pesh. and Ar. as here; at Ps. cvi. 40, Heb., LXX and Pesh. as in the two places just quoted, but the Ar. forsakes them. So far as the word עִבַּת is concerned there can be but little hesitation in adhering to it. It is ἀπ. λεγ. and would be more likely to be altered into a familiar word than *vice versâ*: the Verss. vary so from each other as to excite the suspicion that they had something unfamiliar before them: the sense it yields falls in with the sentiment of the passage as a whole; "The great man utters his own wish and they", the judges and other officials, "twist it" i. e. the cause that is in hand.*
And as to the division of the words some discredit is thrown on the LXX and Pesh. by the violent procedure to which it has driven the former, compelling it to alter the pers. and num. of the verb, as well as by the compulsory omission in both these Verss. of the ה in ויעבתוה, which wants accounting for in some way and, grammatically, would be out of place before טובם. Other reasons will appear for rejecting this arrangement when we turn to v. 4. The rendering of the last part of the verse by Symm. deserves to be mentioned if only for its singularity:

---

* This is preferable to Hitzig's interpretation, according to which the three classes mentioned in this verse "bind together" their diverse interests into one common interest and follow it.

καὶ ὁ μέγας λαλεῖ τὴν ἐπιθυμίαν τῆς ψυχῆς αὐτοῦ, καὶ κατὰ τὰς δασεῖς ἡ δασύτης αὐτοῦ.

V. 4. Probably כַּמְּסוּכָה for מִמְּסוּכָה and מְצַפֶּיךָ for מְצַפֶּיךָ.

טוֹבָם כְּחֵדֶק יָשָׁר מִמְּסוּכָה. Connecting this, as has already been mentioned, with the final word of v. 3, the LXX runs καὶ ἐξ. τὰ ἀγ. αὐτ. ὡς σὴς ἐκτρώγων καὶ βαδίζων ἐπὶ κανόνος. For חֶדֶק no doubt they read חָרָק (Ryssel), rendering it by σὴς and adding ἐκτρ.; they then supplied καὶ, rendered יָשָׁר as a verb and *possibly* read בַּמְשׁוּרָה: to this must be added that the next two words of the Heb. text were joined to this clause and treated as adv. accus., ἐν ἡμέρᾳ σκοπιᾶς σου.* The Pesh. partially agrees with this: "Denique abominati sunt probitatem suam tanquam pannum tineâ corrosum." This is from כח' ישר במ' or perhaps כְּחָרָק אֲשֶׁר בַּמְּסוּכָה. Both these translations are so forced and unnatural that we are compelled to decide against them: whether it is the speaker or the moth, what meaning, at all suitable to the context, can be assigned to β. ἐπὶ κ.? And how, in any such sense as is here wanted, can they abhor their own good, "tanquam pannum &c."?

The Targ. has: "The good man amongst them, it is as hard to get out of his hands as from a thorn, and he who is upright amongst them is more hurtful than the

---

* The Ar. closely renders the LXX, except that it mistook the last word for σκωρίας. The Polyg. ought to have rendered the Ar. as it has done the LXX, not "tineam devorantem," but "tinea devorans." On the σου see below.

enclosure of a destructive hedge."* This is plainly founded on the M. T. The Vulg. does not greatly differ from it: "Qui optimus in eis est, quasi paliurus, et qui rectus, quasi spina de sepe." On the *et* no remark need be made. For the rest it is almost certain that the מ was taken partitively and the *quasi* supplied as demanded by the sense. But this *quasi* indicates a true perception of the requirements of the passage: מ would be very harsh in this place seeing that no adjective such as קשה has occurred in the first comparison: and out of כ, if it was original, the מ of M. T. and the ב of LXX and Pesh. would readily come. Symm. has ὁ ἀγαθὸς αὐτῶν ὡς ἄκανθα, ὁ ὀρθὸς ὡς ἐξ ἐμφραγμοῦ. It is far from unlikely that the כ is original.

יום מצפיך פקדתך באה. The text of the LXX must be considered before we can discuss its rendering. As it now stands we have ἐν ἡμέρᾳ σκοπιᾶς. Οὐαὶ αἱ ἐκδικήσεις σου ἥκασιν in B, but A, Ar. and Jer. repeat the οὐαί. Comparison of this with the M. T. and the other Verss. throws no light on the οὐαί, and there can be no doubt that Roorda is right when he restores as the original LXX σκοπιᾶς σου αἱ ἐκ. κ.τ.λ. The σ of σου has been confounded with the final letter of the preceding word, οὐαί has thus been formed and the αἱ before ἐκ. restored: in A, Ar. and Jer. the process has been carried a step further and οὐαί repeated. In joining ἐν ἡμ. ἐκ. σου to the foregoing clause the LXX were probably influenced

---

* The Polyg. translates the Targ. very badly here, and is especially in error in joining בָּישׁ to the יום of the next clause.

by the difficulty of making both 'פְּקֻד and 'מְצַפּ dependent on יוֹם: the Pesh. and Targ. did not feel this to be insuperable and the Vulg. (see below) did not think it needful to construe thus. The resulting αἱ ἐκδ. σου ἥκ. of LXX is too disconnected to recommend the arrangement: and the τὸν καιρὸν τῆς ἐπισκοπῆς σου of St. Luke xix. 44, which must be a reminiscence of our passage, supplies evidence of a traditional Jewish rendering, similar to that of the Targ., which connected יוֹם with 'פק as well as with 'מצ. In view of the sing. in the other Verss. we need not think that ἐκ. implies a plu. in the Heb. text from which it was rendered: it only brings out the several acts in which the ἐκδίκησις will be accomplished. The Targ. has "dies in qua bonum expectabas, tempus visitationis malitiae tuae pervenit": מטת, the verb, is construed, *ad sensum,* with the governed noun סעורת, corresponding to 'פקד, and not with יוֹם: like the Vulg. and LXX it took כִּצְפִּיךָ as sing. noun with suff.; see Gesen. § 93, 9, Rem.: it supplied עדן (the καιρόν of the quotation in St. Luke) from יוֹם. The Vulg. has "Dies speculationis tuae, visitatio tua venit," which again reminds us of Symm.: ἐμφραγμοῦ ἐν ἡμέρᾳ τῶν προσκοπευόντων σοι. ἡ ἐπισκοπή σου ἦλθε. The sing. fem. noun 'פקד is thus made the subj. to באה, and this procedure, together with that of the Targ., is a strong testimony to the form of the verb here. Only the Pesh. renders כִּצְפִּיךָ as meaning "watchmen": Sebök refers to Jer. vi. 17 and Ezek. iii. 17, and says that the Pesh., more correctly than M. T., read יוֹם צָפִיךָ, the מ of 'מצ being due to dittography. There is no need to follow this opinion: if צָפָה is used in this sense, so also is מִצְפֶּה, and the abstract noun corresponds better to the following פק׳. This latter fact, combined with the consideration that מצפיך would be more readily pointed מְצָפֶּיךָ than מִצְפֶּיךָ, and yet was pointed מְצַפֶּיךָ by LXX and Targ., makes it almost certain that we should adopt the abstract noun here. As to the gender of the suffix, which Sebök rightly feels might be expected to be fem., it must be noted that he does not propose to alter the gender again in the next word. He proposes, however, to change that word. For ܦܩܘܕܬܗ he substitutes ܦܩܕܬܗ, and adduces for comparison Hosea ix. 7. The change is unnecessary, and finds no support in Rich., Add. or Eg., and the passage to be compared does not sustain the cause for which it is advanced: ܦܩܕܢ does indeed occur in it, but it is as a translation of שִׁלֻּם, and פְּקֻדָּה is used in the Heb. of that verse but is rendered by ܡܟܒܠ. Just as little is to be said for the suggestion which has been made that the Pesh. is merely transliterating a פרק which it found or imagined to be in its text. This has originated in the quite obvious fact that the Pesh. here differs from the others in taking the word unambiguously in a good sense: no doubt it was wrong in this, but the word פְּקֻדָּה itself might as well be used in a good as in a bad sense.

עתה תהיה מבוכתם. LXX νῦν ἔσονται κλαυθμοὶ αὐτῶν, Symm. νῦν ἔσται κλαυθμὸς αὐτῶν, and Pesh., "mox erunt funera eorum", derive מבוכה from בכה. The Targ. derives it from בוך and renders it by עֲרָבֻי. The Vulg. has "nunc erit vastitas eorum," and Jerome's note on this runs "sive obsidio: MABUCHA enim magis πολιορκίαν et φρούρησιν, id est *obsidionem* et *custodiam*, quam vastationem in Hebraeo sonat." Ryssel gives a far-fetched and unnatural account of Jerome's procedure here: "darnach verwechselte er מבוכה mit מבוקה das Nah. 2, 11 in der Bedeutung *Leere,* Oede vorkommt, dieses letztere aber wiederum mit מצוקה, Bedrängniss." A reference to Exod. xiv. 3, where נְבֻכִים is rendered "coarctati sunt," shows that his method was much simpler: he believed that this root really meant "to shut in." πλανῶνται, by which the LXX render נבכים in Exodus, shows that they were not unaware of the true meaning of the word: elsewhere they have κλαίω and ταράσσω. It must be added that none of the other Verss. is able uniformly to resist the natural tendency to connect the forms of this word with בכה: at Esth. iii. 15 and Joel i. 18 this is not to be wondered at: in both these places, as well as in Exodus, the Targ. uses one or other form of ערבל, a very apt rendering: at Isa. xxii. 5 the Targ. has קטול, which leaves us in doubt as to whether they thought of בוך or בכה.

V. 5. No alteration.

The asyndeton in the M. T. is preferable to the "and" which all the Verss. use before the second clause. The same remark applies to the "and" with which the Pesh. alone begins the second half of the verse. The plurals φίλοις and ἡγουμένοις do not imply corresponding Heb. plurals: they bring out the sense of the indefinite sing. which is found in M. T., Targ. and Vulg. The Pesh. has been unnecessarily explicit in adding the suffix pronoun כם to each word. ἡγουμένοις of LXX and *duce* of Vulg. are unsuitable to the context, which requires "one near and dear to us," the קריב of Targ. and Pesh. The Vulg. is the only Vers. which has literally translated the next words: "ab ea, quae dormit in sinu tuo." The LXX, ἀπὸ τῆς συγκοίτου σου, the Pesh., "Et ab uxore tua," and the Targ., "ab uxore foederis tui," are all euphemisms. The Vulg. also compares favourably with the rest in its treatment of the final words: "custodi claustra oris tui" preserves the natural image of keeping guard over the doors of the mouth, i.e. the lips. מִלֵּי of Targ. and Pesh. is a feeble substitution of the literal for the figurative, not to be accounted for as the result of an endeavour to obtain a noun corresponding better to the verb. And φύλαξαι τοῦ ἀναθέσθαι τι αὐτῇ of the LXX comes from the mistaken view that in פתחי the infin. occurs.

V. 6. No alteration.

Aiming at symmetry the Pesh. put the suffix pronoun after "father": none of the other Verss. did so. The Lond. Polgy., following *b*, begins this verse with the simple ארי: another recension is represented by *a* and *r* which add הוא בעידנא. The Targ. specializes the meaning of קמה by using מנציא, "wrangles with," and in the next clause adds a verb, מקילא in *b*, מקלה in *r*, מתקלא מקלא in *a*: of these מקלה is a Hebraizing of מקלא, *a* is a confluence of two alternative renderings, and *b*, the fem. part. Aph. of קיל, is probably original. The LXX text of the final clause is somewhat uncertain: B has ἐχθροὶ πάντες ἀνδρὸς οἱ ἐν τῷ οἴκῳ αὐτοῦ; A ἐχ. πάν. οἱ ἀν. οἱ ἐν τῷ οἴκ. αὐτ.: Ar. agrees with A; Jer. has the simpler "inimici hominis viri domestici ejus," and this is like the quotation, St. Matt. x. 36, καὶ ἐχθροὶ τοῦ ἀνθρώπου οἱ οἰκιακοὶ αὐτοῦ: the original probably was ἐχ. ἀνδρὸς οἱ ἐν τῷ οἴκ. αὐτ.: this was strengthened by the addition to ἐχ. of πάντες, which did not interfere with ἀνδρὸς in B, but in A's exemplar ἄνδρες, having been written by mistake, has naturally been put after οἱ and the second οἱ added.

V. 7. No alteration.

b and *r* begin the verse in precise accordance with the Heb. *a* has the אמר נביא with which v. 1 also opens. For ביהוה the usual במימרא דיי is found here. Whilst the other Verss. correctly render אצפה and אוחילה, the Targ. has אבוע and אדוץ. The explanation is to be found in two facts. On the one hand a comparison of such passages as Isa. xliv. 23, xlix. 13, lii. 9, lxi. 10, shows that בוע and דוץ were used as synonyms for translating such verbs of rejoicing as הגיל, &c. On the other hand the Targumist was unfamiliar with the precise idea expressed in our verse, an idea quite suitable to the context, and was misled by his familiarity with the passages where rejoicing in God is the theme; the Targ. on Hab. iii. 18 contains the very words employed here ואנא במימרא דיי אבוע אדוץ לאלהא עביד פורקני.

LXX, Pesh. and Vulg. treat לאלהי ישעי as though the first word were אלהים and the second in apposition to it: so also at Ps. xxv. 5: at Hab. iii. 18 the LXX and Pesh. do so, but the Vulg. has "in Deo Jesu meo," and in

the note on our passage Jerome puts " sive Jesum meum."
At Ps. xxv. 5 the Ar. forsakes its model and renders
according to the Heb. The Pesh., characteristically, puts
" and " before the final clause.

V. 8. No alteration.

b has תחדון, *a* תחדין, *r* תחדן רומי : the original no
doubt is found in *a*; *b* is a scribe's error; *r* is *defective*
and its רומי, which it has in common with the first Vene-
tian Edition and Levita, is clearly a late addition. איבתי
here and at v. 10 is cited by Chwolson * as one of the
examples of the ancient participial fem. ending תִי־ .
None of the Verss. treat it as such, and the suffix furnishes
a much more suitable meaning both here and at v. 10
than the bare " O enemy " would supply. And it is
to be observed that the other examples which he gives
differ from איבתי not only in that some or all of the
Verss. rightly understood them as participles, but also in
that they are all followed by an infin. or a direct object or
a preposition, whereas this word has no such accompaniment, and if it were meant for the participle would necessarily cause ambiguity : at 2 Kings iv. 23 the Verss. regarded הלכתי as partic. and it is followed by אליו ; at Isa.
i. 21 LXX and Vulg., not Targ. and Pesh., took it as
partic. and it is followed by משפט ; at Hosea x. 11 Pesh.
and Targ., not LXX and Vulg., took אהבתי as partic.
and it is followed by לדוש ; at Jer. xxii. 23 all the Verss.
took ישבתי, which is followed by בלבנון, and מקננתי, which

---

* Hebraica, 1890, p. 108.

is followed by ארזים, as participles; and at Jer. li. 13, where the Verss. recognise the partic. in שכנתי, it has על מים רבים after it.

The LXX, Vulg. and Targ. have failed to perceive the parallelism and force of the two כי: ὅτι πέπτωκα is made the cause of the rejoicing, and the second כי is rendered doubly by διότι ἐάν; similarly the Vulg.: "Ne laeteris, inimica mea, super me, quia cecidi: consurgam, cum sedero &c."; and the Targ. has ד in the first place and ארי in the second. The Pesh. perceived the parallelism but did not succeed in expressing the force, using ܘ and ܡܐ. Before ἀναστήσομαι the LXX put καί and, for a like reason, to bring the verb into its necessary prominence, the Pesh. has ܩܘܡܬ. The figurative "when I sit in darkness" is baldly turned into prose in the Targ. ארי יתיבת כדבקבלא. The noun אור, in the Vulg. *lux*, in the other Verss. is represented by a verb: they can scarcely have thought they had a verb before them, seeing that the Hiph. would have been required, but they have given the sense. The rendering by φωτισμός at Ps. xxvii. 1, where Vulg. has *illuminatio*, shows that the noun was known.

V. 9. No alteration.

Corresponding to אמר נביא of v. 1 and in *a* of v. 7, the Targ. begins this verse אמרת ירושלם, to which *a*, by a copyist's error, adds כם. Its perfect קבלית perverts the meaning: its מן קדם and קדם are familiar methods of avoiding expressions that might seem to bring God unduly near to man's level: like ܚܫܘܟܐ of the Pesh. its לוט is used by metonymy of effect for cause, and is chosen, as are the expressions just named, from a sense of reverence. These two Verss. recognise the force of the preposition in בצדקתו: in the next verse the LXX and Vulg. also bring out its meaning. A and B of LXX have καὶ before ἐξάξει: Jerome has it before ὄψομαι also: in the Sixtine text of the Vulg. the Heb. asyndeta are followed, but in the Comm. *et* is found (probably under the influence of the accompanying translation of the LXX) both with *educat* and with *videbo*: Pesh. has it before both verbs: Targ. follows M. T.: Baer and Delitzsch have a note which shows that the Heb. text came under the same kind of influence:—" אֶרְאֶה E 1. 3. habent וְאֶרְאֶה repugnante Masora, quae hanc vocem quinque a Vau copul. incipientibus non adnumerat." ἀπολσει of A, not followed by Ar., is a transcriber's error.

V. 10. No alteration.

LXX and Vulg. have read תְּכַסֶּה and taken בושה as accus. The Targ. and Pesh. agree with M. T. Usage, and the sense of the passage, are rather in favour of the latter. The order of the words, predicate, object, and subject, which has been adhered to in the Targ. and Pesh., may have contributed to mislead the LXX. ותחזי of *b*, as against יתחזון of *a*, is no doubt correct: ותהזי רומי in *r* exhibits the added רומי. A, Ar. and Jer. have πρός με, which is not found in B. It may have been omitted from the original LXX, אלי being so like the next word איו, and afterwards inserted under the influence of the Heb. For איו יהוה אלהיך the Targ. has "Where art thou that art redeemed by the Word of Jahweh thy God?"

Judging from this, compared with Jer. ii. 6, 8 and Joel ii. 17, it would seem that the Targumist on the Prophets avoids a question which would imply the possibility of Jahweh's absence. This is not the case in the Poetical Books, e.g. Ps. xlii. 3, 10. Ryssel, unnecessarily, gives אָן a pregnant sense, "Wo ist, dass du erlöst wirst &c." The usage in the other passages shows that we need not adopt this. For תראינה בה the LXX has ἐπόψονται αὐτήν, Vulg. "videbunt in eam," and the Targ. יחזון במפלתה *. The Pesh. has ב, like the Heb., and the Polyg. translator of it introduces "laeti", which he might with equal propriety have used in v. 9.

V. 11. No alteration.

There can be no hesitation in following M. T., Targ., Pesh. and Vulg. in their treatment of the first half of this verse: they only differ in unimportant particulars, and the sense they give recommends itself, whereas the LXX is an impossible statement. But it is by no means easy to see how the LXX translation arose. For יום לבנות גדריך it has ἡμέρα † ἀλοιφῆς πλίνθου ἐξάλειψίς σου, and it takes the next words into this clause, †ἡ ἡμέρα ἐκείνη. For לבנות they must have read לְבֵנוֹת and looked on this as the plu. of לבנה, although לבנים is the regular form; "the day of bricks" has then been interpreted as "the day when the bricks are used for building by having mortar spread upon them," and this particular word for

---

* b במפלתהון, a and r במפלתה(א).

† ἡμέρας of A can only be a copyist's error, and the omission of ἡ ἡμ. ἐκ. by Jerome's LXX is in all probability an emendation.

expressing it, ἀλοιφή, has been chosen because of the ἐξάλειψις which follows; for גדריך it is possible that some other word, גרד, גדע or גרע may have been read, but there is no binding necessity to assume this. The Vulg. is "Dies, ut aedificentur maceriae tuae": the Targ. בעדנא ההיא יתבנין כנשתא דישראל: the Pesh. "Dies est reficiendi macerias tuas": Symm. ἡμέρα τοῦ οἰκοδομῆσαι τοὺς φραγμούς σου.

יום ההוא ירחק־חק. It is much more in accordance with the genius of the Heb. language to make this a separate clause than to treat it as the LXX, which begins with the first יום of the verse and makes the clause end with this יום ההוא. And the words as they stand give a tolerable sense: "On the day of the building of thy walls the boundary shall be extended." The Pesh. omits חק and renders as though תרחק were the verbal form: "it is the day when thou shalt be carried away." But we can scarcely delete the word on its authority or because of the possibility that it may be a mere reduplication of the final letters of ירחק: the other Verss. all bear witness in its favour, and Jerome's testimony to it as a fully-established reading amongst the Jews is very clear: "ut Symmachus et Theodotio interpretati sunt, dicentes, ἐπιταγὴν καὶ πρόσταγμα.... Hoc sibi Judaei usque hodie pollicentur, et, in eo loco, in quo nos exposuimus: *in die illa longe fiet lex*, sicut nobis visum est et sicut prudentiores eorum disserunt &c." The words of Symm., thus referred to, are: ἐν τῇ ἡμέρᾳ ἐκείνῃ μακρὰν ἔσται ἡ ἐπιταγή. The Targ. has: "in tempore illo irrita fient decreta gentium." This may be from רקק, but it is not absolutely necessary to suppose that they had not רחק before them. The LXX καὶ ἀποτρίψεται νόμιμά σου ἡ ἡμέρα ἐκείνη takes in the first words of the next verse in place of the words properly belonging to this clause and standing at the head of it. The plu. νόμ. and the pron. σου are obviously renderings according to what was deemed the sense, like the ἐξαλειψίς which precedes and the *decreta gentium* of the Targ.: if ἀποτρίψεται of B is genuine it must have originated in דקק being mistakenly read. But there is considerable difference between the form of ירחק and that of ידק; A has ἀπώσεται which in any case is a correction occasioned by reference to the Heb. and apparently is found in Jerome's LXX which he renders "repellet"; but the Ar. read its LXX as ἀποτρέψεται, and if this be the original reading there is no need to assume any other verb than רחק. Aq. and Theod. agree with the LXX in joining יום הוא to ירחק־חק: the former has μακρυνθήσεται ἡ ἀκρισία τῆς ἡμέρας ἐκείνης and the latter μακρυνεῖ πρόσταγμα ἡ ἡμέρα ἐκείνη.

V. 12. For וְעָרֵי מָצוֹר read וְעָרֵי מָצוֹר, and for הָהָר read מְהֵר.

יום הוא ועדיך יבוא למני אשור. The LXX, as we have just seen, is in error in attaching the first two words to v. 11. The rest it renders καὶ αἱ πόλεις σου ἥξουσιν εἰς ὁμαλισμὸν καὶ εἰς διαμερισμὸν Ἀσσυρίων. For עדיך they read עריך, and Ryssel is unquestionably right in saying that they vocalized לִמְנִי and supplied the ל before אשור, treating this letter as infin. Pi., and rendering it by εἰς ὁμαλισμὸν. He is also correct in his account of the εἰς συγκλεισμὸν, *in conclusionem*, which Jerome had, and several MSS. have retained: it is a translation of לִמְנִי מָצוֹר, and has found its way into the wrong place. The Syro-Hexaplar Vers. would seem to indicate* that Ἀσσυρίων was not in the original LXX text, but came in later from the other Greek translators. The Vulg. literally renders the M. T., "In die illa et usque ad te veniet de Assur." The Targ. is also a free rendering of the M. T. בעדנא ההיא יתכנשון גלותא דמן אתור, the verb being put in the plu., as so often in the Targ., and as the LXX and a various reading of the Heb. preserved in the Massora, "סבירין יבואו". The Pesh. is in substantial agreement with the Heb., except that it read עתך for עדיך as at iv. 8.

וערי מצור. LXX καὶ αἱ πόλεις σου αἱ ὀχυραί. Vulg., as if ועד ערי מ׳, "et usque ad civitates munitas." The Pesh., "et ab urbibus munitis," inserts the very opposite preposition, but resembles the Vulg. in feeling that a preposition is wanted. The Targ. differs from the LXX only in not inserting σου, which in the LXX is due to the influence of the first clause. There can be no doubt that Ges., Fuerst, Delitzsch and others are right in holding מצור to mean Lower Egypt. A specification of place is wanted to correspond with "Assyria," and our word should be rendered "Egypt" here and in the next clause, as well as at 2 Kings xix. 24, Isa. xix. 6. In the next clause ולמני מצור has been very variously handled. The Targ. has treated מני in the same way as at Jer. ii. 27, taking it

---

* When Ryssel says it *proves* this he is exaggerating.

to mean Armenia, וְדִמַן חוּרְמִינִי, and has added the epithet רַבְתָא: before מָצוֹר it, like the Vulg., "et a civitatibus munitis," has supplied the עָרֵי of the foregoing clause, and has varied its rendering so as to get almost the very letters of the text, וְקִרְוֵי צִירָא. The LXX has εἰς διαμερισμὸν ἀπὸ Τύρου. The Pesh. follows this so far as the proper name is concerned, "et a Tyro:" the best commentary on these is supplied by Jerome's note: "Sciamus in Hebraeo scriptum esse MASOR: quod verbum si in praepositionem MA, et nomen SOR, dividatur, de Tyro intelligitur; sin autem unus sermo sit, *munitionem* sonat. Denique omnes περιοχὴν, καὶ περίφραγμα, καὶ πολιορκίαν, non de Tyro ut LXX sed munitionem et ambitum muratae urbis transtulerunt."

B and Jer., Pesh. and Vulg. follow the M.T. וְעַד־נָהָר. The Targ., familiar with the view* that the Euphrates is "the river," has וְעַד פְּרָת. In some MSS. of the LXX a like explanation was given by Συρίας being put into the margin, and this has found its way into the text of A, ποταμοῦ Συρίας. No clearer evidence of the origin of this reading could be afforded than that supplied by the fact that in the text which the Ar. translated the word has got into the wrong place at the very end of the verse.

וְיָם מִיָּם וְהַר הָהָר. Not finding לְמִנִּי here the Targ. has treated all these words as under the government of the foregoing וְעַד: מִיָּם it has explained in the very common acceptation of one of the points of the compass,

---

* e.g. 1 Kings iv. 24: at 2 Sam. viii. 3, the Kethib has נָהָר, but the Qeri adds פְּרָת, like the Targ. here.

וימא מערבאה, and the last words it varies from only in using the plu. constr., וטורי טורא. B and Jer. render καὶ ἀπὸ θαλ. ἕως θαλ., καὶ ἀπὸ ὄρους ἕως τ. ο., as though the phrases were formed with the same regularity as those earlier in the verse. The Vulg. is equally regular, but takes the prepositions in reverse order, and renders as though for ההר it had מהר: "Et ad mare de mari, et ad montem de monte." In A and the Ar. there is a double rendering of the last words: after ἀπὸ τ. ὀ. ἕως τ. ὀ. comes ἡμέρα ὕδατος καὶ θορύβου: some one perceived the unsatisfactoriness of the ordinary rendering as compared with the Heb. and wrote the above words in the marg. as an alternative, believing, apparently, that the Heb. should be יוֹם מַיִם וְהָמוֹן: this, as usual, found its way into the text. The Pesh. has "Et a mari usque ad mare," like the LXX, but it vocalized the next words in accordance with Num. xxxiv. 7, "et usque ad montem Hor."

It is impossible to read this verse without coming to the conclusion that the text is corrupt. Unfortunately the Verss. help us very little, and lend scarcely any countenance to the conjectural emendations which one is tempted to make. The following arrangement involves perhaps the minimum of change with the maximum of improvement: יום הוא ועדיך יבוא למני אשור ועדי מצור ולמני מצור ועד־נהר וים מים והר מהך. We cannot adhere to עריך because it is impossible to make this noun the subject to the verb "to come," even if the plu. of the verb were read, and it is impossible to treat it, in its present well-authenticated position, as a *terminus ad quem:* we need not read the plu. of the verb, the indefinite sing. being quite satisfactory: we can understand the perplexity caused to the Verss. by למני because of its rareness: we obtain an excellent sense by altering ערי to עדי, "from Assyria even to Egypt," and the Vulg. shows its feeling that עד or עדי is needed here. We cannot, with Roorda, adopt the "Mount Hor" of the Pesh., seeing that the parallelism with ים מים has some claim on us: and, although the preposition of motion from precedes that of motion to in the other clauses, and occupies the same place here in LXX and Pesh., this may well have been a conformity intentionally brought about, whereas a slight variation of this kind is quite natural and here is testified to by Targ., Vulg. and the ἡμ. ὑδ. κ. θ. of LXX. ה and מ are two letters which are frequently confounded with each other, and it is more natural to believe that there has been such a confusion here than to accept Hitzig's view that the מ of מים is felt, though not expressed, in ההר.

V. 13. No alteration.

For σὺν τοῖς κατοικοῦσιν αὐτήν of B and Ar. μετὰ τῶν κατοικούντων αὐτῶν is found in A, the αὐτῶν being no doubt a copyist's error occasioned by the two previous endings being των. The difference in the prepositions is due to על not being clearly understood, and we can see in the other Verss. that some little difficulty was experienced on this account. The Pesh. has ܠ, making a Dativus Incommodi. The Vulg. makes no distinction between it and the following מן, rendering both by *propter*. LXX and Pesh. render פרי by the plu.; Vulg. and Targ. by sing. But the Polyg. translator gives *ob fructus* for the latter. The translator of the Pesh. is also in error in rendering this verse as a circumstantial clause, and in inserting *illa*: " cum versa fuerit terra illa." There is no need for either of these departures from the simple assertion contained in the text. On ἐπιτηδεύματα, see ii. 7, iii. 4.

V. 14. No alteration.

As in v. 7 *a* again begins the verse with its rubric, אמר נביא. ἐν ῥάβδῳ σου is the original LXX, found in B and Jer. Not satisfied with this rendering of בשבטך some one who knew Heb. wrote in the marg. φυλήν σου: this came into the text of A, which Ar. follows, and its σου led to the omission of the σου after ῥάβ. The nom. αἱ ἡμέραι is somewhat surprising; we should have expected a recognition of the adv. accus. contained in כימי עולם, especially when the next כימי is rendered κατὰ τὰς ἡμέρας. Accordingly Field's note is: " Alia exempl. κατὰ τὰς ἡμέρας. Sic xii. (in marg.), 22, 23, 36, alii, Hieron, Syro-hex." The Pesh. is not content to let צאן stand in apposition to עמך, but inserts "and." If our present reading is correct, it substituted צאן for יער, and read כ before it. Seböks remark is, " Ich kann hier nur wie auch 5, 7 ܠܰܝܳܐ in ܟܒ݂ verwandeln." But the MSS. to which reference has been made do not countenance this change. Like the Targ. the Pesh. takes שכני predicatively, rendering it by 3rd plu. impf. All the Verss. treat the word as plu., but it is better to take it as sing. partic. with the archaic י.—see Ewald, § 211, *b*; Gesen. § 90, 3, *a*. A masc. partic., referring to the fem. צאן, does not surprise us: such constructions *ad sensum* are common.

The Targ. and Pesh. agree in rendering בשן by מתנן; in other passages of the Targ. this is the prevalent form, but at Ps. lxviii. 22 בותנן occurs, and the Pesh., which in several other places has the Heb. form ܟܒܢ, there has ܟܒ ܓܝܐ. We are reminded by these forms of the modern El-Buttein. For בשבטך the Targ. substitutes במימרך, and for the figurative צאן the literal עמא: after "the people of thine inheritance" it adds as an adverbial qualification of פרנס the words "in the world which is about to be renewed": the rest of the verse it renders, "They shall dwell alone who were scattered* in the wood, they shall live in Carmel,* they shall pasture in the land of Bashan and Gilead as in the days of old."

The least satisfactory feature about the M. T. and also the Verss. is the division of the clauses in this verse. The Targ. evades some of the difficulties by freely supplying the verbs which it deems necessary: the Ar. and, it would seem, Jerome's LXX also, reduces the latter part of the verse to an absurdity: "in medio Carmeli pascentur Basanitin et Galaaditin." Cheyne's arrangement of the verse commends itself not only by the excellent sense obtained in the latter half, but also because it avoids the unwelcome order according to which שכני governs יער yet has לבדד between itself and its object: the second half of the verse begins at יער: "in the wood in the midst of Carmel let them feed, in Bashan and Gilead as in the days of old."

---

* *b* and *r* read בחורשא, *a* כח׳: *r* has יתפ.-נסון, *b* and *a* ויתפ׳

V. 15. For אַרְאֶנּוּ read הַרְאֵנוּ.

To connect this more obviously with the last words of v. 14 the LXX and Pesh. begin with "and." A, B and Ar. do not render ארץ, and probably this omission is original: before מצרים the similar מארץ would easily be dropped: in Jerome's LXX it had been inserted, probably through reference to the Heb. The Pesh. had the plu. "days" in v. 14 but has "day" here, to mark the one great historic event. The Polyg. translator has rendered the plu. of the Targ. by "Juxta diem."

In the second clause the imper. is required: it is the continuation of the prayer begun in the former verse, the results of the answer coming in the next. The two כ׳ are thus coordinated, and the harshness of a sudden change to an address of the people by God is avoided. In this connection it is much more likely that *His* coming out of Egypt should be mentioned than that *theirs* should be brought in, and there are many parallels to that thought. The Targ. and Pesh. avoid it, using *מפקהון: they feared to seem anthropomorphic: for אראנו they have אחזנון. The LXX forsakes the Hiph. and employs the 2nd pers. sing. plu. ὄψεσθε. Ewald, § 122, *a*, and § 141, is of opinion that אַרְאֶנּוּ is original, and was a weakened form of הראנו: in a writer of Micah's date this is doubtful, and הראנו should be restored.

---

* So *b* and *r*: in *a* מסקהון; the latter is less likely seeing that Pesh. is ܢܒܗܐ.

V. 16.   For אָזְנֵיהֶם read וְאָזְנֵיהֶם.

This verse also begins with "and" in the Pesh. for the same reason as the preceding one. B has καταισχυνθήσονται καὶ: A, Ar. and Jer. agree with M. T. in not having καὶ, and it is doubtless a mistaken reading caused by the ται of the verb. B has χεῖρας ἐπὶ τὸ στόμα αὐτῶν; so also Ar. and Jer.; A corrects according to the Heb. into χεῖρα ἐπὶ σ. αὐτ. Targ. and Pesh. have "*their* hands ... *their* mouth." The Sixtine Vulg. has "manum super os," but Cod. Amiat. has "manus," and the Comm. "manus suas." None of these imply any other reading than our יד על־פה: they are fuller expressions of the sense. It is not easy to understand how the Polyg. could have felt justified in translating ܡܢ of the Pesh. by *cum*, "cum tota fortitudine sua." They seem to have wrongly interpreted the "might" as that of the heathen and therefore have done violence to the word in question.* It is also a distinct fault in the rendering of the Targ. that no note is taken of the ו before אודנהון: the Pesh. agrees with the Targ. in having the conjunction, and A of the LXX has it. Baer and Delitzsch's note on the Heb. text runs: "Lectionem Orientalium, qui ו addunt, sequitur, ut solet, Chaldeus." And there is some MS. authority for it: E 3 reads it and E 2 likewise, "sed adjiciens in margine, פליגא (i.e. *controversum*). Etiam in B prima manu scriptum erat וא attamen Vav obliteratum." It ought to be admitted into the text,

---

* In Jerome's Comm. the same interpretation occurs: *in omni fortitudine sua*, qua vastaverant quondam et praevaluerunt adversus populum Dei."

for this is not one of the cases where asyndeton adds force; rather does it create obscureness.

V. 17. No alteration.

For ὄφεις, which must be original, ὄφις was mistakenly or through reference to the Heb. written in some MSS. A and Ar. have the sing.; Jer. has the plu. The Ar. escapes from the difficulty in which its sing. would otherwise have placed it by employing for σύροντες a finite verb parallel to λείξουσι. זחלי is not a common word, and it did not appear probable to the LXX translator that a second comparison would be likely to follow in which a less specific word describing the same kind of creature would be used. He therefore took כזחלי 'א as being in apposition to כנחש and did not think it needful to render the כ. But the second clause begins much better with כ, which thus gets its own verb; the other Verss. support this, and the Pesh., after its manner, marks off the new clause by "and." For ממסגרתיהם the ordinary MSS. of the LXX followed by Ar. have ἐν συγκλεισμῷ αὐτῶν; Jer. ἐν συγκλεισμοῖς αὐτ. The Vulg. has "in aedibus suis." Targ. and Pesh. retain the מן, which certainly is original: רגז מן means "to flee trembling from," and this is a much more picturesque image than "to tremble in." With reference to the plu. συγκ. found in Jer., there can be no doubt that it is an emendation made for the sake of conformity to the Heb.: at the same time it is not probable that the LXX read the Heb. as sing.: it is using a collective in place of a plu. The Pesh. word, ܫܒܝܠܝܗܘܢ, "paths," is used also by the Pesh. as a rendering of the same word at 2 Sam. xxii. 46, Ps. xviii. 46: at the latter place it is noteworthy that the LXX has ἀπὸ τῶν τρίβων and the Vulg. "a semitis": at 2 Sam. xxii. 46, on the other hand LXX is ἐκ τῶν συγκλεισμῶν and Vulg. "in angustiis." There is a singular rendering of the first clause of this verse in the Targ., ישתטחון על אפיהון על ארעא כחויא. Were they ashamed to reproduce the inexact statement that serpents lick the dust? If so they have substituted for the figure the fact which corresponds to it. In such passages as Isa. xlix. 23, Ps. lxii. 9, where there is no reference to the serpent, they reproduce the Heb. לחך.

In the second half of the verse the Pesh. is peculiar in commencing with "and" as well as in omitting the closing ממך: with the former procedure we are very familiar; the latter is no doubt due to their unwillingness to use the second pers. of the Being who in the same clause has been spoken of in the third pers. Like the Pesh. the Targ. here avoids the use of אל with the verb of fearing, in fact it renders both the אל and the מן by מן קדם: it is observable that at Hosea iii. 5 they do not seem quite at home with this construction, ופחדו אל־יהוה being rendered by them ויתנהון לפולחנא דיי and ܣܢܝܒܝܢ ܒܡܪܝܐ. The inexact יתברון וידחלון for יפחדו ויראו reminds us of 1 Sam. xvii. 11, where ויחתו ויראו is rendered ואיתברו ודחילו.

V. 18. No alteration.

The Targ., as well as the Pesh., turns the question with which the verse opens by a negative assertion, though not in quite the same way, the former having, "There is none beside Thee, Thou art the God who forgivest &c.;" the latter, "There is none, O God, like Thee, who forgivest &c." On this method of procedure, see note to v. 10. ἀνομίας (or as A has it ἀδικίας), ἀσεβείας, τοῖς καταλοίποις, are the plurals for collective singulars of which we have met so many; the Targ., too, has חובין and עוין. The Pesh. alone renders as though for עבר the Hiph. were to be read: "He removeth the transgression." The Vulg. alone has *tuae*, keeping to the second pers. because of the "Quis Deus similis *tui?*" LXX and Pesh., as so frequently, begin the second half of the verse with "and." The LXX vocalizes לְעֵד, εἰς μαρτύριον: the sense of the expression might have been expected to prevent this. Jerome's note is: "Ubi nos interpretati sumus, *non immittet ultra furorem suum;* pro ultra, Symmachus transtulit, *in sempiternum;* Theodotio, *in finem:* Septuaginta et Quinta Editio, *in testimonium:* pro quo positum est in Hebraeo LAED." This shows that his own somewhat peculiar "ultra" is not from any other word than that in the M. T., and the explanation of its employment is to be found in the verb "immittet" which it modifies: "non immittet ultra" is another way of putting "He will not retain for ever." There is no need to render the Targ. רעי לאיטבא הוא, as Ryssel does: he takes איט as meaning "das gottgewollte Thun der Menschen": "placet ei beneficia conferre" is much better. And there can be little doubt that in harmony with this the Pesh. here is, as in Lond. Polyg., ܛܒܘܬܐ, not ܬܝܒܘܬܐ; "beneficence" is much more in place than "penitence."

Sebök says: "Die P. Ausgabe von Lee. 1823, liest
ܐ݇ܒܕ̄ܝ ܚܛܐܬܢ̈ܐܕ ܥܠܘ̈ܗܝ: es ist wohl ܚܛܐܗ̈ܘܢܕ zu lesen.
Die Verderbniss ist entweder in Folge einer phonetischen
Täuschung entstanden, oder dadurch, dass der untere Theil
des ܢ verwischt war (vgl. P. zu חסד im letzter Verse
&c.)." In the last verse we have ܢ.

V. 19. No alteration.

A begins this verse with αὐτός, a rendering of the הוא
at the end of v. 18, and the Ar., which ends that
verse with ھو, commences this with وهو. Roorda holds
that αὐτός belongs to the original text of the LXX: it is
more likely that it was a later addition due to some one
who did not see that הוא had already been translated by
ἐστίν. Almost of necessity the LXX, which is followed
by Pesh. and Vulg., inserts καὶ before οἰκτειρήσει, but the
καὶ before καταδύσει which is found in A, the Pesh. and
the Targ., not in Ar. or Jer., is not required. These
first words ישוב ירחמנו יכבש עונתינו are enlarged by the
Targ. into יתוב מימריה לרחמא עלנא ויכבוש על חובנא
ברחמתיה. For 'יכ' עונ the Pesh. is ܢܒܘܫ ܟܠܗ ܚܘܒܢ.
This, if correct, must have originated in a deliberate adoption
of כנש, the Aramean form of the ordinary Heb. כנס, in preference to כבש for the sake of suitableness to the next
clause: the sins are first gathered together, and then cast
into the sea. Ryssel and Sebök accept this. It is, however, to be noted that at Jer. xxxiv. 16 and Zech. ix. 15,
the Pesh. has ܟܒܫ.

B has the grammatically impossible καὶ ἀποῤῥιφήσονται
εἰς τὰ βάθη τῆς θαλάσσης πάσας τὰς ἁμαρτίας ἡμῶν, and

Jer. supports this. A, several other MSS., the Syro-hex. in textu, and the Ar. have ἀποῤῥίψει, which no doubt is original, ἀποῤῥιφήσονται having arisen from ἀποῤῥίψει εἰς τὰ, or else having been a marginal reading, written first by some one who perceived that the 3rd per. sing. did not accord with his Heb. text, and afterwards finding its way into B without effecting the needful alteration to πᾶσαι αἱ ἁμ. The latter is the more probable explanation. The remaining Verss. agree with the LXX, both as to the person of the verb and as to that of the suffix pron., except that the Targ. has חטאי ישראל. This exception suffices to show that the Targ. read with the M. T. חטאתם, and I think we are bound to adhere to this as well as to ותשליך: it is much more likely that the Verss. have departed from the Heb. text for the sake of conformity with the foregoing words, than that the reverse change has been made in the Heb. And, on the other hand, the whole of the passage from v. 17 to v. 20 is so full of alternations from predications concerning God to direct addresses to Him that we can feel no surprise at the second person here. The suffix of the 3rd pers. in חטאתם may also be a preparation for the 3rd perss., Jacob and Abraham, which immediately follow. With regard to the form of the verb, E 3 writes ותשלך, and the Massora Parva confirms this, noting ours as the only place where the word is written defectively. The Vulg. "profundum" has no doubt come from מצלת having been written without vowel letters: at Zech. x. 11, where מצולות is found in the M. T. as compared with מצלות here, the Vulg. is *profunda*: but it is to be observed that Jerome's LXX is here rendered by him *profundum*, and there *profundu*. Curiously the Targ. עומקי is translated *profundum* in the Polyg. of our passage.

V. 20. No alteration.

If our present LXX text, which is supported by Jer. and Ar., is correct, the verb which opens this verse was altered like תשליך from the second to the third pers., and for the same reason. But this alteration is not followed by the other Verss. It is, however, not at all unlikely that the δώσεις which is found in some codices* is original: δώσει εἰς ἀλήθειαν is a curious expression and may easily have come by mistaken transcription from δώσεις ἀλ.: there is no preposition before ἔλεον corresponding to the εἰς: and the sec. pers. ὤμοσας follows at once. The καθότι of LXX and כמא of Targ. is a very natural way of treating אשר, and does not imply a reading כאשר. The מימי of M. T. and the other Verss. is more suitable than the כימי which the LXX seem to have read.

The Targumist takes the opportunity of rounding off the work by bringing in as fully as possible the history of the fathers, the oath at Beth-El, the Covenant made when Abraham divided (בתר Gen. xv. 10) the animals of the sacrifice into pieces, the binding (עקד Gen. xxii. 9) of Isaac preparatory to his being offered. All these go to form the treasury of merits which Israel may plead before God: "Thou wilt give the truth of Jacob to his sons as

---

* "22, 23, 36, alii."—*Field*. Aq. Symm. and Theod. also have 2nd pers.

Thou didst swear unto him in Beth-El, the kindness* of Abraham to his seed after him, as Thou didst swear to him between the pieces. Thou wilt remember on our behalf the binding of Isaac who was bound upon the altar* before Thee. Thou wilt perform with us the kindnesses* which Thou didst swear to our fathers from the days of old."

---

* *a* has וטבות but *b* and *r* ט': *b* has נבי מדבחא *a* and *r* omit נבי: *a* adds וקשוט כמא. In all three cases the shorter reading is to be preferred.

LIST OF PROPOSED ALTERATIONS.

Chap. i. 5. For בָּמוֹת read בֵּית חַטַּאת

      7. For קִבְּצוּ read קָבְצָה

      9. For נָגְעָה read נָגַע

      10. For בָּכוֹ read בַּכּוּ

Chap. ii. 2. For וְאִישׁ read אִישׁ

      4. For נָהָה נְהִי לֵאמֹר read נָהָה נְהִי נִהְיָה אָמַר; for יָמִיר read יָמַד; for לִי read לוֹ

      6. For יַטִּפוּן read נָטוֹף: prefix כִּי to the לֹא of the last clause: for יִסַּג read יַסֵּג

      7. For הַיָּשָׁר הֹלֵךְ read הָאָמוּר: for הֶאָמַר read הַיָּשָׁר הָלְכוּ

      8. Write וְאֶת־מוּל for יְקוֹמֵם read יָקוּם: for אָדָר: for שְׁבוּרֵי either שׁוּבֵי or שְׁבִי: for אַדֶּרֶת read

      9. For נְשֵׁי read נְשִׂיאֵי

      10. For תְּהַבֵּל וְחֶבֶל read תְּחַבֵּל חֶבֶל

      12. For בָּצְרָה read בְּצָרָה

Chap. iii. 3. For שְׁאֵר עַמִּי אָכְלוּ read וּשְׁאָר עַמִּי אָכְלוּ: for כַּאֲשֶׁר read כִּשְׁאָר

      6. For חֲשֵׁכָה read חָשְׁכָה

      10. For בֹּנֶה read בָּנִים

Chap. iv. 8. Omit תָאתָה

    13. For וְהַחֲרַמְתִּי read וְהַחֲרָמְתְּ

Chap. v. 1. For אֶפְרָתָה צָעִיר read אֶפְרָתָה הַצָּעִיר: omit לִהְיוֹת

    3. For וְיָשָׁבוּ read יָשְׁבוּ and attach it to the middle clause of the verse.

    4. For כִּי־יָבוֹא אַשּׁוּר read אַשּׁוּר כִּי־יָבוֹא

    5. For בִּפְתָחֶיהָ read בִּפְתִיחָה

    12. & 13. These should be read as one verse, as follows:—

וְהִכְרַתִּי פְסִילֶיךָ וּמַצֵּבוֹתֶיךָ וְנָתַשְׁתִּי אֲשֵׁרֶיךָ מִקִּרְבֶּךָ וְלֹא־תִשְׁתַּחֲוֶה עוֹד לְמַעֲשֵׂה יָדֶיךָ:

Chap. vi. 9. For וְתוּשִׁיָּה יִרְאֶה שְׁמֶךָ read וְתוּשִׁיָּה לְיִרְאֵי שְׁמוֹ

    11. אֶזְכֶּה need not be altered, but it is another form of יִזְכֶּה

    16. For עַמִּי read עַמִּים

Chap. vii. 3. For לְהֵיטִיב read הֵיטִיבוּ

    12. For וְעָדַי מָצוֹר read וְעָרֵי מָצוֹר: for הָהָר read מֵהָר

    15. For אַרְאֶנּוּ read הַרְאֵנוּ

    16. For אָזְנֵיהֶם read וְאָזְנֵיהֶם

LIST OF ALTERATIONS FOR WHICH A FAIR DEGREE OF PROBABILITY MAY BE CLAIMED.

Chap. i. 5. חַטֹּאות for הַטָּאת

iii. 8. וּמִשְׁפָּט וּגְבוּרָה is probably an early gloss.

iv. 14. שָׁמוּ for שָׁם

vi. 5. Before הַשִּׁטִּים insert וּמֶה־עָשִׂיתִי

16. וְיִשְׁתַּמֵּר for וְיִשָׁמְרוּ

vii. 4. כִּצְפִּיךָ for מְצַפֶּיךָ and כִּמְסוּכָה for כִּמְסוּכָה

Williams (T. S.) Modern German and English Conversations and Elementary Phrases, the German revised and corrected by A. Kokemueller. 21st enlarged and improved Edition. 12mo. cloth 3s

Williams (T. S.) and C. Cruse. German and English Commercial Correspondence. A Collection of Modern Mercantile Letters in German and English, with their Translation on opposite pages. 2nd Edition. 12mo. cloth 4s 6d

Hickie (W. J.) Easy German Reading-Book. With Outline of Grammar, etc. 8vo. cloth 1s 6d

Apel (H.) German Prose Stories for Beginners (including Lessing's Prose Fables), with an interlinear Translation in the natural order of Construction. 2nd Edition. 12mo. cloth 2s 6d

German Classics for English Schools, with Notes and Vocabulary. Crown 8vo. cloth.

Grimm's Hausmärchen, by W. J. Hickie 2s
Schiller's Lied von der Glocke (The Song of the Bell), and other Poems and Ballads, by M. Förster 2s
────── **Minor Poems.** By Arthur P. Vernon 2s
────── **Maria Stuart**, by Moritz Förster 2s 6d
Goethe's Hermann und Dorothea, by M. Förster 2s 6d
────── **Iphigenie auf Tauris.** With Notes by H. Attwell. 2s
────── **Egmont.** By H. Apel 2s 6d
Lessing's Minna von Barnhelm, by Schmidt 2s 6d
────── **Emilia Galotti.** By G. Hein 2s
Chamisso's Peter Schlemihl, by M. Förster 2s
Andersen (H. C.) Bilderbuch ohne Bilder, by Beck 2s
Nieritz. Die Waise, a Tale, by Otte 2s
Hauff's Mærchen. A Selection, by A. Hoare 3s 6d

Fouque's Undine, Sintram, Aslauga's Ritter, die beiden Hauptleute. 4 vols. in 1. 8vo. cloth 5s
Undine. 1s 6d; cloth, 2s.   Aslauga. 1s 6d; cloth, 2s
Sintram. 2s 6d; cloth, 3s. Hauptleute. 1s 6d; cloth, 2s

Latin, Greek, etc.

Cæsar de Bello Gallico. Lib. I. Edited with Introduction Notes and Maps, by ALEXANDER M. BELL, M.A. Ball Coll., Oxon. Crown 8vo. cloth   2s 6d

Euripides' Medea. The Greek Text, with Introduction and Explanatory Notes for Schools, by J. H. Hogan. 8vo cloth   3s 6d

—— **Ion.** Greek Text, with Notes for Beginners Introduction and Questions for Examination, by the Rev. Charles Badham, D.D. 2nd Edition. 8vo. 3s 6d

Platonis Philebus. With Introduction and Notes by Dr C. Badham. 2nd Edition, considerably augmented 8vo. cloth   4s

Dr. D. Zompolides. A Course of Modern Greek, or the Greek Language of the Present Day. I. The Elementary Method. Crown 8vo.   5s

---

Kiepert New Atlas Antiquus. Maps of the Ancient World for Schools and Colleges. 6th Edition. With a complete Geographical Index. Folio, boards   7s 6d

Kampen. 15 Maps to illustrate Cæsar's De Bello Gallico 15 coloured Maps. 4to. cloth   3s 6d

---

Spanish.

Harvey (W. F.) Practical Spanish Manual. Grammar, Exercises, Reading Lessons, &c. Crown 8vo. cloth 4s 6d

---

Italian.

Volpe (Cav. G.) Eton Italian Grammar, for the use of Eton College. Including Exercises and Examples. New Edition. Crown 8vo. cloth (Key, 1s)   4s 6d

Racconti Istorici e Novelle Morali. Edited, for the use of Italian Students, by G. Christison. 12th Edition. 18mo. cloth   1s 6d

Rossetti. Exercises for securing Idiomatic Italian, by means of Literal Translations from the English by Maria F. Rossetti. 12mo. cloth   3s 6d

—— **Aneddoti Italiani.** One Hundred Italian Anecdotes, selected from "Il Compagno del Passeggio."

www.ingramcontent.com/pod-product-compliance
Lightning Source LLC
Chambersburg PA
CBHW020826230426
43666CB00007B/1117